THE HOLY LAND

A Pilgrim's Companion

by

David Baldwin

To this Holy Land:
'Peace-through-Justice,
And Glory-through-Devotion.'
(*Ba* 5:4)

*All booklets are published thanks to the
generous support of the members of the
Catholic Truth Society*

CATHOLIC TRUTH SOCIETY
PUBLISHERS TO THE HOLY SEE

Photography

All Photographs courtesy of Israelimages.

Acknowledgements

Grateful thanks to Rev Kevin Robinson, Sr Elizabeth Rees OCV and CTS Readers.

CONTENTS

∾ FOREWORD ∾

Recently I made a fervent plea for Christians to go on pilgrimage to the Holy Land. This was not only for their benefit but also for the benefit of the Christian people of the Holy Land, many of whom had suffered much hardship because of the continuing conflict there. So I am very pleased to commend *The Holy Land - a Pilgrim's Companion*. David Baldwin has written an excellent booklet with maps, photos and prayers and with simple commentaries on the places where Jesus fulfilled his ministry. This booklet will help all visitors to the Holy Land not only to learn about the places where Jesus ministered but also to enter in prayer and reflection on his life, death and resurrection. Thus, a visit to the Holy Land becomes truly a pilgrimage of the disciples of the Lord. I warmly commend this booklet and sincerely hope it will be a true companion for very many pilgrims.

Cormac Cardinal Murphy-O'Connor
✠ Archbishop of Westminster

∾ WHERE JESUS WALKED ∾

A Pilgrim Land

Of all Christian pilgrimage destinations, the Holy Land must surely be the most desired. This is not a conjectural or wistful statement, but one that is backed by the presence and witness of the countless millions of pilgrims who have continuously journeyed there - during the bad times as well as the good - and still do, over the two millennia of Christian history. Since the first day of that empty Tomb - where a miraculous Resurrection from an ignoble and miserable death was witnessed and reported - pilgrims have gone to that sacred spot to ponder, wonder and believe. And from that place, many pilgrims, in Origen's words, wished also "to walk in the footsteps of the Master", to visit and meditate in those places where Jesus lived, moved and carried out His ministry. Of course, the ebb and flow of the pilgrim numbers was very much dictated, and still is, by the prevailing conditions of that Land: the wars that rage, the attitude of the conquerors and occupiers towards Christians and Christian pilgrims.

In Pope John Paul II's words, as he contemplated his historic visit to the Holy Land in the Jubilee Year of 2000, "It is a witness which sets me in a long

procession of people, who for 2,000 years have gone
in search of the 'footprints' of God in that land,
rightly called 'holy', pursuing them as it were in the
stones, the hills, the waters which provided the setting
for the earthly life of the Son of God.... How many
pilgrims, how many saints, have followed these paths
down the centuries! Even when events in history
disturbed the essentially peaceful nature of pilgrimage
to the Holy Land, giving it an aspect which, whatever
the intentions involved, was hard to reconcile with the
image of the Crucified One, more sensitive Christian
souls sought only to find the living memory of Christ
on that soil".

This book is offered as your invitation and stimulus
to actively join that 'long procession of people', to go
and walk in those footprints, to seek that 'living
memory'. But in seeking the Divine inspiration of the
past, we can also, together with our own Church
leaders, go and publicly support and encourage today's
beleaguered Christians, many of whom are Palestinians,
who happen to live in and around that area. The reward
of doing so will be immense: the awe of discovering
and immersing yourself in that sublime past, the joy of
sharing the present with fellow Christians from all
around the world - but also, giving those Christians who
live there, hope for their future. For without that hope,
and without the support of pilgrims worldwide, there is

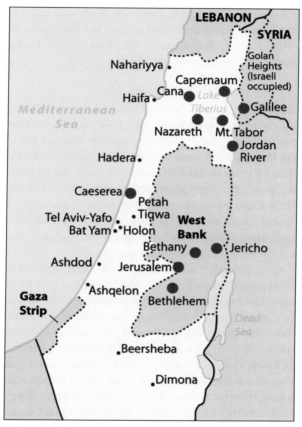

The Holy Land.

a danger that these holy places of Jesus will become completely isolated, fall into disuse, and eventually be relegated to fond memory and folklore.... Those footprints blowing away into dust....

How to use this book

The purpose of this small book is to take you either as journeying pilgrim, or armchair reader, to this extraordinary, dynamic and spiritually charged place, the Holy Land. Its aim is to facilitate and provide that little bit extra to those who actually make the journey; to convey the atmosphere and spiritual context of the Holy Land to those, who for whatever reason, are unable to go; to rekindle memories and provide new insights to those who have made the journey, and maybe even prompt inspiration to revisit!

It is intended as a handy-sized, self-contained Pilgrim's Companion. In this Introduction a brief historical background is given to set the scene. There is a more detailed timeline at the back; this outlines the sometimes violent ebb and flow of the clashing ownership of the faiths and cultures over the centuries, which have so affected attitudes and concerns throughout the ages, and which still prevail today. It will also help to clarify the chronology surrounding the churches, buildings, places and people that you will encounter.

The sequence of the book follows the pattern of Jesus' life, starting in Nazareth with the Annunciation, going on to the principal places involved with His ministry, and then, to Jerusalem to His death and resurrection. It provides a mix of descriptive and meditative texts and prayers. It also gives relevant Scriptural passages, although it would be wise to pack your Bible, so that in quiet moments you will be able to read more fully about the places you have visited and the events of which you have heard. Provision of information by the many churches and other sites varies enormously: where there is a dearth, this book will at least provide a starting point; where information is available, it will supplement, and may even help you to spot further items of interest.

❧ THE HOLY LAND IS UNIQUE ❧

The faiths of Abraham

Spiritually, one will not only observe at first hand, but may also have to come to grips with the manifestations of this Land as the cauldron of the three great monotheistic faiths. We are all the common sons and daughters of Abraham - each of us very different - perhaps suspicious, certainly ignorant of each other; maybe even scornful and even prejudiced to some degree, but all of us attempting to live and practise our respective faith, whilst hopefully making a conscious effort to respect and understand each others' point of view.

As Christians, our starting point with the Jews - indeed our own attitude as 'the People of God in the New Covenant' - must be to regard the Jewish people as having been the first to hear the Word of God, and that their faith, unlike other non-Christian religions, is already a response to God's Revelation in the Old Covenant. In the words of the Catechism of the Catholic Church (*CCC*), "To the Jews 'belong the sonship, the glory, the giving of the law, the worship and the promises; to them belong the patriarchs, and of their race, according to the flesh, is the Christ; for the gifts and the call of God are irrevocable'. And when

Sunset over Jerusalem.

one considers the future, God's people of the Old Covenant and the new people of God tend towards similar goals: expectation of the coming (or the return) of the Messiah. But one awaits the return of the Messiah who died and rose from the dead and is recognised as Lord and Son of God; the other awaits the coming of a Messiah, whose features remain hidden till the end of time; and the latter waiting is accompanied by the drama of not knowing, or of misunderstanding, Jesus Christ." (*CCC* 839, 840)

With our attitude to Muslims, we must understand, indeed welcome, that: "The plan of salvation also includes those who acknowledge the Creator, in the first place amongst whom are the Muslims; these profess to hold the faith of Abraham, and together with us they adore the one, merciful God, mankind's judge on the last day." (*CCC* 841)

Christian communities

Whilst on the 'macro' front one may experience and witness this diversity of the three faiths, one's antennae may also pick up - on the 'micro' level - with maybe some discomfiture and indeed surprise - that Christians of different traditions rub along together here with a degree of unease, and because of this and its effect, one may have to come to terms with this as well. Key to understanding this are the oscillations of ownership - and jealous retention once received - of the holy sites over the millennia - specific ownership being favoured by the particular brand of occupant and patron of the time - whether it be Byzantine, Crusader, Saracen, British, Israeli.

The principal contentions tended to be between the Western Church of Rome, and the Orthodox Eastern Churches. Sadly, disputes were invariably taken to the highest levels of government - church and state - and as a result, settlement was inevitably a political (and unsatisfactory) compromise. Frustrated by the squabbling churches at the time, division of ownership of the holy places was formally codified by *firman* (decree) of the Open Court (*Sublime Porta*) of the Sultan of the Ottoman Empire in 1767, who was ruling Palestine during that period, and amazing though it may seem, it has not changed substantially since!

Status Quo

These divisions of ownership laid down by the Sultan are known as the 'Status Quo'. In practical terms this has meant dividing a holy site into some discrete single-area ownerships, which in itself causes right-of-way and boundary problems. However, the problems further compound over those areas that cannot be divided, and are designated 'common territory' within a jointly owned church property or building. The overall effect is that agreement over repair, maintenance or development usually stagnates through lack of consent from all ownership communities. This often leads to the neglect of badly needed repairs, as communities simply cannot agree among themselves about the scope and shape of a project. This includes who pays how much and for what - the more offered by one community often being regarded with suspicion as an attempt to gain a larger share of ownership.

A serious and specific reflection of this problem is the badly needed renovation of the edicule (*aedicule* - little house) - the structure containing Jesus' Tomb in the Church of the Holy Sepulchre in Jerusalem (see more details in separate Chapter) - where the need is very pressing, but where any physical changes might result in altering the status quo, which could be disagreeable to one or more of the communities. A more whimsical example is the wooden ladder standing under a window ledge over the church's main entrance. It was put there sometime before 1852 on what is defined by the status quo as common ground; presumably, no-one knows who put it there, and no-one, seemingly, has the authority - or the temerity - to remove it, and it remains there to this day.

Terra Sancta and the Franciscans

Specific Catholic (Latin) ownership of many of the sites is also widespread, with French, German and Italian Orders discretely owning some sites. Predominant though, are the Franciscans, who are charged directly by the Holy See with custodianship of those sites within the *Terra Sancta* - the Holy Land - of which the Cross of Jerusalem (with its cluster of one large and four small crosses) is the prominent and instantly recognisable 'logo'. The history of this ownership goes back to St Francis himself, who travelled to the Holy Land in 1219/20 to visit his Friars who had already established a presence there in 1217. When the Crusaders were finally driven out in 1291 at the fall of Acre, the Franciscans took refuge in Cyprus.

Gradually they started returning, firstly with discreet annual visits, until, in 1322 they regained a presence in the Holy Sepulchre, took ownership of the Upper Room as granted by the Sultan of Egypt in 1333, building a monastery nearby, and in 1347, they settled in Bethlehem at the Church of the Nativity. Their first statutes regarding the Holy Land, dating from 1377, provided that a maximum of twenty friars should serve the Holy Places (Upper Room, Holy Sepulchre and Bethlehem), and their principal activity was to ensure worship in these Sanctuaries and to give spiritual assistance to pilgrims.

Since those times they have continued their unflagging efforts to maintain and develop a Catholic presence, often under very difficult circumstances and sometimes at the price of martyrdom. They have been at the forefront of significant archaeological and historical research in this area, which has led not only to more understanding of our Faith, the Scriptures and the times of Jesus, but to site development in which to express it and take it forward. These many sites that are wholly owned and run by the Franciscans are invariably beautifully presented and impeccably maintained, but be aware that smaller sites may often be closed.

The Franciscans' activities are extensive, going well beyond their original brief, and spreading into many areas of social care and welfare in Palestine. They maintain an important and ongoing interface with the Eastern Churches. Their headquarters is at their monastery in the Christian Quarter of Old Jerusalem, and their church of St Saviour is well worth a visit. The importance in maintaining these holy places, and the Franciscans' activities in the Holy Land, is recognised by the Vatican, who call to the faithful round the world once a year to make their personal contributions in their parish collection plates.

Sharing with the Eastern Churches

Because of the status quo and the proximity of members of the other Christian faiths, your pilgrimage will bring you into close contact with churches and sites of the Eastern Churches - some as owners in their own right, and others, like the Church of the Holy Sepulchre in Jerusalem or the Nativity in Bethlehem, through co-ownership. For us, of the Western tradition, entering these places, we may be forgiven our initial surprise (in my case disappointment) for not having been pre-warned at how totally empty and bare they may appear. They are often devoid of any furniture, devotional ornamentation, colour or decoration, except for the seeming over-profusion of hanging votive lamps and the glittering icons, particularly in the sanctuary area. They can also appear rather shabby, careworn, smoke begrimed, and haphazardly decorated and maintained.

However, one must appreciate that some of this is caused by the limitations of the status quo, but we must also respect what these places represent, and that they are presented in the authentic Eastern Christian tradition. Whilst this may challenge - even test our pilgrim integrity at the time - we must nevertheless close our Western eyes and our prejudices, and see what these places are, whilst also bearing in mind their genuine intent, and in some cases their exceptionally venerable age!

As Roman Catholics, we share a common sacramental inheritance with the Eastern Churches, and as such should welcome and embrace those with whom we have such a strong Apostolic identity. In the words of Pope John Paul II (*Orientale Lumen*), "For us, the men and women of the East are a symbol of the Lord who comes again. We cannot forget them, not only because we love them as brothers and sisters redeemed by the same Lord, but also because a holy nostalgia for the centuries lived in the full communion of faith and charity urges us and reproaches us for our sins and our mutual misunderstandings: we have deprived the world of a joint witness that could, perhaps, have avoided so many tragedies and even changed the course of history."

The Human Mix

To give context to the 'people picture' in the Holy Land, about 9 to 10 million people live here, of whom roughly 5.5 million are Jews, and the remainder Palestinians, with a small fraction of 'others'. Of the Palestinians, about 150,000 are Christian, the rest are Muslim. The principal Christian denominations are: Greek Catholics (Melkites) (67,000), Greek Orthodox (50,000), Armenian Orthodox (2,000), Coptic

Orthodox (1,000), Ethiopian Orthodox (1,000), Syrian Orthodox (1,000), Protestant (4,000). With this in mind, you should also get used to the term used for our Church - Roman Catholics - as the 'Latin Church' or 'the Latins', of which there are about 25,000, most of them Palestinian Arabs. The indigenous Palestinian Christian community has dramatically shrunk over the years, particularly in Bethlehem, going from 85% of the population of 60,000 in 1948 to 12% in 2006.

Pilgrim Challenges

Part of the challenge is to see beyond the popular perception of the Holy Land being in a permanent state of siege and terror; it is this perception that keeps away pilgrims from all over the world in their thousands. However, if we really want to go, we need only apply an intelligent, objective assessment of the situation, based on a very simple rule of thumb: if responsible tour companies and other organisations are operating into the Holy Land, then it must be acceptably safe to go, whilst also consulting the specific advice given by the Foreign Office on their travel website, *www.fco.gov.uk*. I am not by any stretch advocating taking foolish risks or undertaking acts of pious bravado. But it may just be, like the pilgrim of the Middle Ages who set off in faith and trust to walk the hundreds of miles to his pilgrim destination, enduring every hardship and fear that we should also step out of our comfort zone to go on our own special journey, our own memorable pilgrimage in faith and trust. The remainder of the challenge, then, is for you (with a tour group, as a parish, with a diocese) to join together as a band of pilgrims and fulfil that innate desire to walk where Jesus walked - it is not out of reach!

"This I believe: I shall see the goodness of the Lord, in the land of the living." (Ps 27:13)

Security

The many pilgrim sites in and around Jerusalem are easily walkable, obviating the need for transport of any sort whilst there. Some may feel that Israel is over-policed, but by the same token, a security presence, although at times rather offhand or brusque, is ever present.

However, movement in and out of the Palestinian Authority Areas, such as Bethlehem or Jericho, and in the West Bank, is tightly controlled by the Israeli Security Forces, and may at times be limited or curtailed. A major part of this, and one very evident when entering somewhere like Bethlehem, is the 'Separation Barrier', with its watch towers and check points, erected by the Israelis to rigidly control entry and exit from the West Bank and Palestinian Authority areas. This controversial barrier, which very roughly follows the 1949 Armistice Line (Green Line), is planned to be 670 kms long, of which to date 36% has been constructed.

In places near habitation it is a stark, ugly, utilitarian concrete construction, about 8 metres high. It is a blight on the landscape, ploughing blindly through towns, villages, even houses, but far more significantly, it is a blight on the Palestinian people. To the Israelis it is a successful tool in preventing suicide bombers from entering and operating in Israel; to the Palestinians it separates families, suffocates communities, and appropriates land. Experiencing these check points is both a humbling and a humiliating experience: humbling in providing an inkling into what ordinary people are being subjected to every day, and humiliating by the impersonal and casual manner in which one is scrutinised (or ignored!) as one passes through. In going into these areas I certainly felt no threat whilst visiting Christian venues.

Some tips

Something I suggest that you do not become too hung up on are the various claims and assertions that 'on this exact spot, so-and-so happened'. Generally, the tradition (both practical and oral) handed down through generations of believers from those earliest days of how and where these events happened, even during times of persecution and seeming obliteration, is strong. If not on this exact spot, it may have been within a few hundreds of metres, or maybe a kilometre or so, or, in rare instances, a lack of certainty or somewhere else altogether, but does it really matter? As a continuation of earlier oral tradition there is also early written evidence of places and practises, as recorded by early pilgrims, amongst whom are the (anonymous) Bordeaux Pilgrim who went to Jerusalem in 333, and the travels of Egeria, a Spanish nun, who wrote about her visits some fifty years later, about whom we will hear later on.

The other challenge is the familiar one that has to be faced at every major pilgrim site, particularly at peak, busy periods - and that is the noise, the chatter, flashing cameras, hubbub and general feeling of irreverence. Detaching from all this can be difficult, but in attempting to do so, try and consider that every visitor, tourist or pilgrim is on a journey, their journey, and the Lord will walk and work with one and all.

Apart from the guides and other information books (see Bibliography) two very useful and comprehensive sources of information for accommodation, transportation, opening times and events are the

Christian Information Centre run by the Franciscans located by the Jaffa Gate, Old Jerusalem, *www.cicts.org*. There is also a conventional Tourist Information Office just inside the Jaffa Gate.

Seek as a Pilgrim

The key to meeting and facing the challenges posed by the Holy Land, whether they be trying to make your mind up to go, or of making sense of what you experience when you get there, must be through prayer. Through prayer seek to discover more of God, of this still tortured place where Jesus chose to work and die, of the people and faiths who live here, of yourself. Pray for the grace to peel away the layers of human folly, pride and fear (including our own!), and see these places for what they really are. In Pope John Paul II's words, "To go in a spirit of prayer...in the area marked especially by God's intervention, helps us not only to live our life as a journey, but also gives us a vivid sense of a God who has gone before us and leads us on, who himself set out on our path, a God who does not look down on us from on high, but who became our travelling companion," - so, travel on your pilgrimage with Jesus as your companion!

And during those moments when challenges may beset and puzzle you, and prayer may not be so easily forthcoming, it may simply be enough to invoke Peter's innocent and naïve enthusiasm during those marvellous moments of the Transfiguration, when he exclaimed to Jesus, "Rabbi, it is wonderful for us to be here!" (*Mk* 9:5).

What really matters is that these things did happen, Jesus did walk this Land, and we are here to remember, to give praise and thanks, and to draw closer to God through these holy places. In the words of St John of Damascene (6th century):

We venerate those created things
by which, and in which,
God brought about our Salvation.
We venerate all the Holy Sites,
not for their nature,
but because they are vessels
of God's action.

A Pilgrim Blessing

May the babe of Bethlehem be yours to tend;
May the boy of Nazareth be yours for friend;
May the Man of Galilee his healing send;
May the Christ of Calvary his courage lend;
May the Risen Lord his presence send;
And his holy angels defend you, to the end.
(From *'Come, See the Place'*)

THE HIDDEN YEARS

❧ THE ANNUNCIATION ❧

"....the angel Gabriel was sent by God to a town in Galilee called Nazareth." (Lk 1:26)

"The Annunciation to Mary inaugurates 'the fullness of time', the time of the fulfilment of God's promises and preparations. Mary was invited to conceive him in whom the 'whole fullness of deity' would dwell 'bodily'. The divine response to her question, 'How can this be, since I know not man?', was given by the power of the Holy Spirit: 'The Holy Spirit will come upon you'." (CCC 484)

Nazareth Town

In Roman times Nazareth was a small insignificant Jewish town nestling in a valley in lower Galilee. Although it receives no direct mention in the Old Testament, some Biblical scholars link the then inhabitants of Nazareth, the Natzoreans, with the Hebrew for shoot or twig (*netzer*) and tie it in with *Is* 11:1, "A shoot [twig] will spring from the stock of Jesse, a new shoot will grow from his roots". But whatever the expectations of the Natzoreans for the coming of the Messiah, they were seemingly the butt of more sophisticated outsiders, depicted by

Nathaniel's quite blunt response when Philip was telling him about "...him of whom Moses in the Law and the prophets wrote, Jesus son of Joseph, from Nazareth", which was: "From Nazareth? Can anything good come from that place?" (*Jn* 1:45, 46).

But it was from this humble Galilean town that news of the Incarnation of God was given to Mary, the one chosen by God to bear His Son, Jesus. And from this place, and in the person of Mary, came the very first act of Christian faith, and not only the first act, but one demonstrating profound trust and willingness in the face of the complete unknown, when Mary declared, "You see before you the Lord's servant, let it happen to me as you have said" (*Lk* 1:38).

Today, Nazareth is a bustling, sprawling, dusty town of both old and new. Until 1948 it was predominantly Arab and Christian, but since then, a large Israeli settlement was developed as a modern adjunct on the hills above, Nazareth Ilit. That there has been a Christian presence, in the form of Jews who converted to Christianity (proto or Judeo-Christians) since early times, was evidenced by the modern excavations made before the present Basilica was built. These revealed the presence of a pre-Byzantine shrine with some recognisable charcoal incisions of graffiti, proclaiming 'Lord', 'Christ', 'Hail Mary' and many cross motifs.

This shrine was also documented by the historian Africanus in the 3rd century. In the 4th century pilgrimage to Nazareth was further attested by the pilgrim Egeria: "In Nazareth is a garden in which the Lord used to be after his return from Egypt. There is a big and very splendid cave in which she (that is holy Mary) lived. An altar has been placed there, and there, within the actual cave, is the place from which she drew water. Inside the city the synagogue where the Lord read the Book of Isaiah, is now a church." "The desire to faithfully commemorate the place of the Annunciation has been carried through the centuries, beset by the waves of invasion, conquest, bloodshed and destruction so prevalent throughout the region.

Early church

The early Christian village of Nazareth has been excavated by the Franciscans - its remains can be viewed in the plaza above the modern basilica. Two unique baptisteries also survive: one beside the grotto inside the basilica, and the other, with its mosaic floor intact, beneath St Joseph's church, within the basilica complex.

The first major church was Byzantine, built in the early 4th century, attributed to Constantine's mother, Helena, who, in Egeria's words, "turned to Nazareth, and having sought the house, where the Mother of God, all worthy of praise, received the Hail of the Archangel Gabriel, thereat she raised the Temple of the Mother of God". This church was destroyed in 614 by the Persians, over which was built a larger Crusader church in the 12th century. This was razed to the ground in the 13th century by Saladin's armies, although subsequently pilgrims were still given access to the Grotto which was left intact, and which was also venerated by Muslims. The Franciscans established a presence in Nazareth in the 14th century, but it was not until the 18th century that they started building another church over the site of the Grotto. This was subsequently demolished in 1965 to make way for the present Basilica of the Annunciation, the largest church to be built in the Holy Land for nearly 800 years.

THE BASILICA OF THE ANNUNCIATION

This large, modern Basilica, with its clean external lines and gleaming pale stonework, is crowned with a graceful inverted lily-shaped bronze dome, and is prominent in the Nazareth townscape. It was designed by the Italian Giovanni Muzio, and completed in 1969. The apex of the western main entrance façade is dominated by a statue of Our Lord, beneath which, over the whole façade, are clean-cut bas relief scenes and quotations from the Bible, depicting the Mystery of the Incarnation. Stretching the length of the façade, just above the triple doorways, are those words central to the Christian Faith, "The Word became flesh, he lived among us" (*Jn* 1:14).

The spacious, paved external cloister to the right of the west facade is lined with many contrasting mosaic images of Our Lady, donated by Catholic communities from all round the world. Whilst you are on this southern side of the Basilica, note the inscription *Salve Regina*, the welcoming figure of Mary, and the door showing twelve scenes from her life. Going back round to the west entrance now view the impressive main bronze door, depicting six scenes from the life of Jesus. The smaller, side doors show, on the left, the fall of mankind and its consequences, and on the right, three prophecies of redemption from the Old Testament, 2 *S* 7:16, *Is* 7:14, *Ezk* 9:4.

Entrance through these doors takes one into the soft, hushed atmosphere of the lofty, modern cavern of the lower church. The focal point is the sunken area round the Grotto of the Annunciation. It is beautifully and tastefully presented, incorporating, through a graceful wrought iron gate, the grotto cave where the Annunciation is remembered and venerated. Inside is the small altar from the Franciscan church of 1730, and the grotto itself is dramatically flanked by the

Basilica of the Annunciation, western facade.

remnant columns and stonework from the earlier
Byzantine and Crusader churches. Glancing up gives
a direct and striking view of the dome high above.
Light pours in through the crowning lantern,
highlighting the delicate symmetrically veined pattern
of the inside of the 'lily' petals. Attending Mass in
this sunken crypt area, focussing into the tiny sacred
space of the grotto, whilst being embraced by this vast
majestic church, will be a highlight of your pilgrim
journey. Here, we contemplate and meditate on the
Annunciation.

Immediately to the left of the grotto is the
martyrium, or shrine, of a 3rd century martyr, Conon,
with its painted wall plaster and mosaic floor intact.
To the left of the shrine, on the next raised section of
flooring, is the 'wreath mosaic' on which early
Christian baptismal candidates symbolically stood.
This shrine is unique in the Christian world, providing
us with valuable insight into the theology of the early
Jewish Christians.

The Annunciation

*"In the sixth month the angel Gabriel was sent by
God to a town in Galilee called Nazareth, to a
virgin betrothed to a man named Joseph, of the
House of David; and the virgin's name was Mary.
He went in and said to her, 'Rejoice you who*

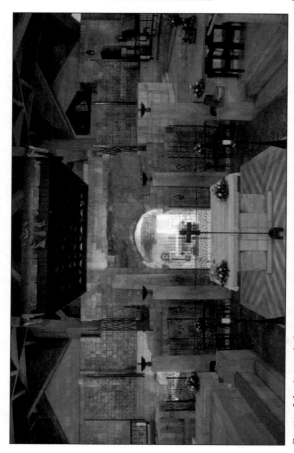

Grotto of the Annunciation.

enjoys God's favour! The Lord is with you.' She was deeply disturbed by these words and asked herself what this greeting could mean, but the angel said to her, 'Mary, do not be afraid; you have won God's favour. Look! You are to conceive in your womb and bear a son, and you must name him Jesus. He will be great and he will be called the Son of the Most High. The Lord God will give him the throne of his ancestor David; he will rule over the House of Jacob for ever and his reign will have no end.' Mary said to the angel, 'But how can this come about, since I have no knowledge of man?' The angel answered, 'The Holy Spirit will come upon you, and the power of the Most High will cover you with its shadow. And so the child will be holy and will be called the Son of God. And I tell you this too: your cousin Elizabeth also, in her old age, has conceived a son, and she whom people called barren is now in her sixth month, for nothing is impossible to God.' Mary said, 'You see before you the Lord's servant, let it happen to me as you have said.' And the angel left her."
(*Lk* 1:26-38)

Here, one can also pray the First Joyful Mystery of the Rosary - the Annunciation.

Upper church

Entry to the upper church is near the main entrance, up a spiral staircase lit with brilliantly coloured glass windows. The surprise on entering the upper Basilica is also of its majestic size and contrasting design, giving it a sense of separate entity from the lower church, were it not for the octagonal aperture at floor level which joins the two and lets the dome's light down into the church below. One's eye is then drawn down the length of the church to the magnificent 150 square metres of mosaic above the high altar, one of the largest in the world, showing in bright, clear and detailed picture the Triumph of the Universal Church. Jesus, arms outstretched with St Peter standing close by Him, Our Lady enthroned at His right hand, all overseen by the hovering Spirit above, and over the whole, the all-seeing eye of the Creator. A myriad of figures from Christendom fading into a far horizon makes up the rest of the mosaic.

The side aisles of the church continue with the theme of images of Our Lady from all over the world. Those who were disappointed in not seeing any contribution from England on viewing the mosaics in the cloister before entering will now have their reward: the full length mosaic nearest to the Franciscan side chapel is Our Lady of Walsingham, in which the Slipper Chapel is also featured. This international Basilica also serves the humble, very practical and necessary purpose of being the Parish Church for the Catholics of Nazareth.

Meditation

The Angel reveals God's expectations for the future of mankind. Mary replies by drawing attention responsibly to her present situation: she is engaged to Joseph, promised as his spouse. Mary does not raise objections to the future prepared by God; she asks for light on the present human circumstances in which she is involved. God responds to her request by entering into dialogue with her. He wishes to deal with persons who are responsible and free. In all this, what is the lesson for us? Mary shows us the path towards a mature freedom. In our days, many baptised Christians have not yet made the faith their own in an adult and conscious way. They call themselves Christians and yet they do not respond in a fully responsible way to the grace they have received; they still do not know what they want and why they want it. This is the lesson to be learned today: an education to freedom is urgently needed.... With the Virgin Mary's example before us, we are invited to reflect: God has a project for each of us, he 'calls' everyone. What is important is knowing how to recognise this call, how to accept it, and how to be faithful to it." (*Pope John Paul II*)

Prayer

Father,
I abandon myself into your hands;
do with me what you will.
Whatever you may do, I thank you:
I am ready for all, I accept all.
Let only your will be done in me,
and in all your creatures.
I wish no more than this, O Lord.

Into your hands I commend my soul;
I offer it to you with all the love of my heart,
for I love you, Lord,
and so need to give myself,
to surrender myself into your hands,
without reserve,
and with boundless confidence,
for you are my Father.
(*Blessed Charles de Foucaud*)

Baptistry and museum

The baptistry is separate from the church, reflecting the early Church's custom of not permitting the unbaptised to enter during the celebration of the Sacred Mysteries. The striking panels of amethyst and green glass represent the baptismal waters. Some oil presses and silos associated with the old village are on display here. The modern-style bronze font shows the baptism of Jesus by John the Baptist. The whole structure is a gift from Germany. On the north side of the baptistry is a system of underground caverns, stores, silos and water systems which existed under the old town in Jesus' time; they link through to the Grotto of the Annunciation.

The Franciscan museum is adjacent to the church, here the most important items are the five historiated capitals intended for the 12th century Crusader church, but which were buried before being installed to escape the destruction wrought by Saladin in the 13th century. They are in pristine condition, being some of the finest examples of 12th century Romanesque art.

CHURCH OF THE HOLY FAMILY

In the same compound as the Basilica is the Church of St Joseph, also known as the Church of the Holy Family, or the Carpenter's Shop. This sturdy modern church, with its elegant, arched bell tower, was built around 1914 in Crusader style and over earlier Crusader foundations, and commemorates Joseph's carpenters shop. It is a simple, plain, unadorned church, in which points of interest are the underground caverns probably dating back to 1000BC, and used as grain silos, and latterly as accommodation and other domestic purposes. Through a wrought iron grille one can view a pit about three metres square with seven steps leading down to a mosaic floor, which is likely to be a full baptismal pool of the 1st-3rd century Judeo-Christian era. Beside it is a cave, in which the early Church candidates for baptism renounced Satan, and were presented with the light of Christ on Easter night.

MARY'S WELL

A short walk from the Basilica, through the crowded, jostling *souk* alleyways, sitting in a small square behind a balustraded stone wall and Roman style arch, is the Greek Orthodox church of St Gabriel, also known as Mary's Well. This compact, plain stone church, with its slim miniature bell tower, houses an ancient spring said to have been serving Nazareth in Mary's time, where she would come daily to draw her water. According to the apocryphal

Gospel of St James, the Angel Gabriel first appeared
here to Mary to declare the Incarnation, and she
being very flustered at this seemingly public
approach, withdrew home, where he re-appeared to
make the Annunciation.

The well, or spring, is found straight through the
small church, down some steps into the crypt, and is
at the end of a low, long vaulted cavern built by the
Crusaders in the 12th century. As you go through,
note the richly decorated Armenian tiles on the vault
walls, put there by the Crusaders. Through the iron
balustrade at the end, one can hear the burble of
flowing water and peer down the stone-lined shaft at
this ancient water source. The church itself is a fine
example of Greek Orthodox architecture, with its
richly iconned *iconostasis* shielding the altar, and its
many ornate, hanging devotional lamps.

Meditation

Water, as the source of life is a powerful,
universal image whose reality is only faced when
it is scarce or runs dry. In the lands of plenty it is
taken for granted: growth is constant, life is not
threatened, lushness and abundance prevail.
Where it is deficient or hesitant, growth is
stunted, famine stalks, and lack of it can mean

death. Either way, through circumstance of birthplace, tribe or family, it is out of our hands, as individuals. But what is not out of our hands is whether we choose to drink of the living water. For Jesus said, "Let anyone who is thirsty come to me! Let anyone who believes in me come and drink!" As scripture says, 'From his heart shall flow streams of living water'" (*Jn* 7:37, 38). From this Divine source the water is plentiful, constant and universal. It is one thing we can always take for granted, but it is up to us as individuals how often we drink, or even if we drink at all - do we wait until we are parched and gulp it greedily until slaked, and then neglect ourselves again? Or do we, in the modern idiom, take our bottle with us wherever we go, and take constant sips to stay refreshed? As we pray and meditate at this ancient water source, we hold in our minds this lovely image - this mysterious paradox - of the young, loving Mother, who had the humbling responsibility of the wellbeing of the Son of God, coming here daily to draw the water that would sustain the life of her precious Son, the Son from whose pierced heart water would gush, giving life to the world.

(*David Baldwin*)

OTHER PLACES

If time permits, there are other places in Nazareth
worth a visit (check accessibility and times with the
Christian Information Centre): the very plain
Synagogue Church, owned by and next to the Greek
Catholic (Melkite) church. This is the site where Jesus
by tradition learned as a boy and preached during His
ministry, and where his fellow townsfolk, 'would not
accept him', to which Jesus' riposte was, "'a prophet is
despised only in his own country and in his own
house', and he did not work many miracles there
because of their lack of faith." (*Mt* 13:57, 58); the
chapel of the Little Sisters of Jesus where Charles de
Foucauld prayed when he worked as a gardener for the
Poor Clares; the Poor Clares have built a new convent
up the lane opposite the Galilee Hotel. Here one can
visit a small museum containing some of Charles de
Foucald's meagre possessions, including some of his
writings and drawings - he was a fine artist.

❧ THE VISITATION ❧

"Now it happened that as soon as Elizabeth heard Mary's greeting the child leapt in her womb and Elizabeth was filled with the Holy Spirit" (Lk 1:41).

In the context of those words, above, "Mary's visitation to Elizabeth thus became a visit from God to his people" (CCC 717).

Ein Kerim

About seven kilometres west of Jerusalem is the village of Ein Kerim, the place where tradition has it that Mary's cousin Elizabeth lived with her priest husband Zechariah, and where Mary visited her cousin with child, soon after the Annunciation. Formerly a pleasant Palestinian village, abandoned in 1948, it is now effectively a suburb of Jerusalem, populated by writers and artists, but it still retains, with its immediate surrounding greenery, a quiet, village atmosphere. It is a place noted for its wild flowers, particularly its deep, purple everlasting flowers which can be found in summer on the roadside banks. In spring, below the Church of the Visitation, one will find wild cyclamen, red anemones, poppies and orchids. There are two churches here: one commemorating the Visitation, and the other the birth place of John the Baptist.

CHURCH OF THE VISITATION

This attractive, Franciscan church is set on a rocky
hillside, its pale stone work contrasted by the dark
green of the surrounding cypress trees; an elegant bell
tower and spire gives it height. The church is on two
levels; the lower level being the remains of Byzantine
and Crusader buildings, and the upper, modern
church, built to Barluzzi's design, started in 1938 and
consecrated in 1946, finally being completed in 1955.

Before entering one will notice the large mural on
the west façade, of Mary, riding a donkey on her way
to visit Elizabeth; there is also a delicate wrought iron
screen at the entrance to the courtyard. Around the
courtyard is displayed the Magnificat in over forty
different languages.

The cloister arches lead from the courtyard directly
into the lower Chapel. Inside, and opposite the entrance,
is an ancient tunnel leading to an old well. Tradition
tells of the waters joyfully springing out of this rock
when Our Lady greeted Elizabeth. Three large,
colourful frescoes on the chapel walls show Zechariah
in the Temple, the Visitation, and the Slaughter of the
Innocents. Below this fresco is a niche displaying a rock
known as the Stone of Hiding, where according to the
2nd century 'Testimony of James' Elizabeth concealed
John the Baptist from Herod's soldiers.

Ein Kerim - Church of the Visitation.

Outside again, to a set of steps to the left of the cloister arches that lead to the upper Church. There is no doubting as to whom this Church is dedicated - it is a glorious depiction of Our Lady (and women from the Old and New Testament) not only through her time on earth, but throughout subsequent history. The five large paintings on the south wall take us to the Council of Ephesus where Mary was declared the Mother of God, to Mary the Protector of the Church, the miracle at Cana, the battle of Lepanto, where Mary's intercession through the Rosary secured victory for Christian forces against the Turks in 1571, and lastly, to Blessed John Duns Scotus (d. 1308) defending the Immaculate Conception before the Sorbonne. The centre painting in the apse is that of the church being dedicated to Our Lady by the Patriarch and the Franciscan Custos of the Holy Land.

This is a very lovely, tranquil church and setting in which to reflect, pray and meditate.

The Visitation

"Mary set out at that time and went as quickly as she could into the hill country to a town in Judah. She went into Zechariah's house and greeted Elizabeth. Now it happened that as soon as Elizabeth heard Mary's greeting, the child leapt in her womb and Elizabeth was filled with the Holy

Spirit. She gave a loud cry and said, 'Of all women you are the most blessed, and blessed is the fruit of your womb. Why should I be honoured with a visit from the Mother of my Lord? Look, the moment your greeting reached my ears, the child in my womb leapt for joy. Yes, blessed is she who believed that the promises made her by the Lord would be fulfilled'." (Lk 1:39-45)

Meditation

Those few words above, written by Luke, contain a treasury of emotions and images evoked by the meeting of these two joyful, holy women:

Courage.... *'Mary set out at that time'* ... having just experienced the most amazing angelic announcement that she had been chosen to be the Mother of God and was now with child... yet she had the trust and guts to get out and face the world....

Selflessness.... *'went as quickly as she could'* ....one of her first actions is to set forth straight away, to share Elizabeth's joyful news...not hers!

Encounter..... *'the child leapt in her womb'* .... This most amazing encounter between Jesus and John the Baptist was the spiritual pre-figuration of the public meeting of the two, some thirty years later in the desert, with John proclaiming, '...Look there is the lamb of God that takes away the sin of the world...' (*Jn* 1:29), and affirming, 'I have seen and I testify that he is the Chosen One of God' (*Jn* 1:34).

Faith..... *'blessed is the fruit of your womb...'*....Elizabeth's completely spontaneous and intuitive outburst that the Son of God was present in Mary's womb, is a clear demonstration as to what Faith should be...spontaneous, intuitive, strong, uninhibited (*'she gave a loud cry...'*), trusting...and maybe without realising it at the time...profound.

Humility.... *'...why should I be honoured with a visit from the mother of my Lord?'*....through her faith, Elizabeth has no doubt as to Jesus' presence in Mary's womb, and humbly bows before her young cousin....and the unborn Lord.

Joy.... *'...the child in my womb leapt for joy...'*....there was also no doubt in Elizabeth's mind as to her son John's reaction to this extraordinary meeting...a somersault of pure exaltation. Joy is also a conspicuous theme of the whole event as is evident from the words and actions of both women.

Wonder.... *'Yes, blessed is she who believed that the promise made her by the Lord would be fulfilled'*...again, Elizabeth had no doubt that what

Mary had told her of the extraordinary events of
the Annunciation were utterly true and were
worthy - through her faith - of unconditional belief.
Love.... the whole encounter, between these two
mothers, and their unborn children, is charged with
such love for each other, their babies, and above
all, the Lord their God.
(*David Baldwin*)

Here, one can also pray the Second Joyful Mystery
of the Rosary - the Visitation.

CHURCH OF ST JOHN THE BAPTIST

*"The time came for Elizabeth to have her child,
and she gave birth to a son; and when her
neighbours and relations heard that the Lord had
lavished on her his faithful love, they shared her
joy."* (*Lk* 1:57,58)

Close to the centre of the village is the church of St
John the Baptist, which by tradition is the location of
St John the Baptist's home and birthplace, and the
home of his parents, Zechariah and Elizabeth. It is a
sturdy, rather blunt looking church, with its fortress-
like appearance in the Crusader style. There is

evidence of 5/6th century chapel buildings on the site, which were subsequently built over by the Crusaders in the 11th century. Although this building fell into disuse and disrepair after the Crusaders had left, it still forms the basis of the current church. The Franciscans had access in the 15th century and finally secured ownership of the site in the 17th century, and started repairing it, of which ongoing additions were made in the 18th and 19th centuries. The rebuilding process was supported mainly by the Spanish Royal Family, of which a distinctly Spanish flavour can be detected throughout the church.

Entrance to the church courtyard is through an arch decorated with the Jerusalem Cross and the Franciscan 'crossed arms' symbol. On one of the exterior walls of the church are twenty three tile plaques (with the twenty fourth round the corner) displaying the *Benedictus* (*Lk* 1:68-79) in different languages - the prayer that Zechariah said on the naming of his son John, and the universal prayer of the Church said every day at Morning Prayer. Beneath the steps that lead up to the church one can peer through some basement windows covered with twisted iron bars through to the floor of the original Byzantine church. This contains an early martyrs' chapel (4-7th centuries) with a fine mosaic floor, decorated with crosses, partridges, peacocks, and pomegranates.

Although quite gloomy inside the modern church above, one can soon make out the six massive pillars separating the three aisles, and their high dado of distinct blue and white tiles brought from Valencia. The church resounds with many works of art, including those by Murillo and Ribalta, all gifts from the Spanish people over the centuries. Probably the most striking are the gilded three dimensional Stations of the Cross, with their chapel-shaped wooden frames, vibrant colours and intricately detailed facial expressions. Five statues dominate the central apse. To the left, Zechariah, in his garb of a priest of the Temple with St Elizabeth on the other side. Towering above them both is Our Lady; on either side of the apse is St Francis of Assisi and St Clare.

From inside the church, through an ornate green and gold gate and down some steps, is the *Benedictus* Grotto. This is where St John's birth is commemorated. Beneath the small altar is a brightly lit carved marble medallion with the inscription, *'Hic precursor Domini natus est'* ('Here was born the precursor of the Lord'). The altar was made in Livorno and donated by Queen Isabella of Spain. The floor is the original 11/12th century of multi coloured *opus sectile* (larger, mosaic shaped 'jigsaw' pieces). There are also some interesting items on display: beautifully embroidered vestments, superb candlesticks, gold and silver vessels,

splendid ancient icons and the *'comunichino'*: tongs
used for distributing the Holy Communion to people
suffering from the plague.

Homecoming

*"Mary stayed with her some three months and then
went home." (Lk 1:56)*

Bible commentators have observed that Luke's habit
was to 'round off one episode before passing to the
next' - which was John's birth in the next verse. It is
thought likely, however, that Mary would have stayed
with Elizabeth for the birth and circumcision of John
the Baptist - the time scales certainly support this -
before turning for home to Nazareth. There she would
prepare for the birth of her own child in circumstances
that she could not have imagined, but would accept in
great strength, trusting submission and total faith.

❧ THE NATIVITY ❧

"Today in the town of David a Saviour has been born to you; he is Christ the Lord" (*Lk* 2:11).

"At the time appointed by God, the only Son of the Father, the Eternal Word, that is, the Word and substantial Image of the Father, became incarnate; without losing his divine nature he has assumed human nature" (*CCC* 479).

Ancient Town

Bethlehem, an ancient town, 8 kms south of Jerusalem, and some 170 kms from Nazareth, often features in the Old Testament. It was the home of David the shepherd boy (c1004-965 BC), where he was anointed by Samuel: "Yahweh said to Samuel....I am sending you to Jesse of Bethlehem, for I have found myself a king from among his sons" (1 *S* 16:1 ff). The prophet Micah (8C BC) foretold the birth of Jesus, "But you (Bethlehem) Ephrathah, the least of the clans of Judah, from you will come for me a future ruler of Israel..." (*Mi* 5:1 ff).

There are two accounts of the birth of Jesus in the New Testament in Matthew and Luke. But because of the suppression of the First (AD 70) and Second (AD 135) Jewish Revolts by the Romans, Jews were proscribed from living in this area, and as such, very little physical evidence from the first to the third centuries has subsequently come to light. However, oral tradition of the birth must have been very strong - we can imagine the shepherds passing down this wondrous event to their children and grandchildren: '...when they saw the child they repeated what they had been told about him...', (Lk 2:17), and undoubtedly with local people marvelling over the visit of the magnificent Magi to this humble babe!

Cave of the Nativity

That the birth was in a cave is very strongly supported by history. In 135, the Emperor Hadrian ordered that a grove, dedicated to the pagan god Adonis, be planted to detract from this cave marking the birth of Christ. As early as 155, Justin Martyr from Nablus records, "Should anyone desire proof for the birth of Jesus in Bethlehem....let him consider that, in harmony with the gospel story of his birth, a cave is shown in Bethlehem where he was born, and a manger in the cave where he lay wrapped in swaddling clothes".

Origen confirmed this in 215, and Eusebius, Bishop of Caesarea, similarly at the end of the third century. Around this area, St Helena, Constantine's mother, ordered the building of a magnificent Basilica in 323. By the end of the fourth century it was a well

established place of pilgrimage. The desert to the east
became one of the great centres of Byzantine
monasticism, indicating the depth of Christian
devotion in this region. In 386, St Jerome settled in
Bethlehem; from here he translated the Bible into the
Latin vulgate, it being accepted as the authoritative
version used by the Western Church at the Council of
Trent. Initially interred there, his remains were
subsequently moved to St Mary Major in Rome.

THE BASILICA OF THE NATIVITY

The original Basilica was largely destroyed during the
Samaritan revolt of 529, but on the same site and very
soon after, the Emperor Justinian ordered the building
of a larger Basilica, incorporating what remained of
Constantine's church. Unusually for this war-torn and
ravaged part of the world Justinian's Basilica was
spared further destruction, and still stands today. That
it survived the Persian invasion of 614 (where most
other churches in the Holy Land were destroyed) is
down to one of the mosaics on an interior wall. A 9th
century Greek document attests "[when the Persians]
arrived at Bethlehem, they saw with awe the figures
[on the mosaic] of the Persian Wise Men, star-gazers,
their country folk. For the respect and love towards
their ancestors they revered them as if they were still

alive and spared the church. That is why it is still standing today".

On approaching from Manger Square, there is nothing overtly 'church-like' about the group of buildings you see in front of you - it is more like a mediaeval fortress complex, with its forbidding, solid stone walls and few, small high windows. Immediately on the right of the square is the Armenian convent with its rather squat modern bell tower, further along is the much larger Greek Orthodox convent tower, and over to the left of the square, the tower of the Latin Church. The entrance to the Basilica of the Nativity at the back of the square is not very Basilica-like either - it is tiny, only admitting one at a time at a stoop. An examination of this entrance reveals through the external stone-workings an ever diminishing size of door over the ages, with the practical purpose of preventing, in the 17th century, horse and cart being taken into the church to remove the proceeds of looting! Nowadays it is known as the Door of Humility, as all but children have to bow their head on entering this holy place.

Inside

The church, owned jointly by the Armenians and Greek Orthodox, is presented in the Eastern tradition, and appears totally bare, devoid of any furniture, devotional ornamentation, colour or decoration, apart

Church of the Nativity - Door of Humility.

from a profusion of hanging oil lamps, and the rich *iconostasis* decorating the sanctuary and main altar. It is a long, tall, lofty church with a simple, timbered and gabled roof; light enters from the round-arched clerestory windows high above. The double rows of eleven sturdy columns of local white-veined red sandstone support and create the space for the wide nave and aisles. Twenty eight of them have the dim remnants of 12th century paintings on their surfaces; high up on the walls there are fragments of splendid 12th century mosaics with which the Crusaders lavishly adorned the church, the best example being 'Doubting Thomas' in the north transept. The simple, paved floor has some wooden trap doors set in it, which open to reveal lower level sections of 5th century mosaic of the original floor.

The first Crusader king, Baldwin I, was crowned king of Jerusalem here on Christmas Day in 1101, preferring Bethlehem over Jerusalem, in refusing to be crowned with gold in the city where Christ was crowned with thorns.

Grotto of the Nativity

"No one, whether shepherd or wise man, can approach God here below except by kneeling before the manger at Bethlehem and adoring him hidden in the weakness of a new born child." (*CCC* 563).

Grotto of the Nativity.

Entry to the Grotto of the Nativity is from the right
hand (east) transept close to the *iconostasis* of the
high altar. The side chapel and altar in this transept is
Greek Orthodox, commemorating the Circumcision of
Jesus. Going down the stairs, built by the Crusaders,
one enters the Grotto, which in busy periods can seem
quite cramped and distracting - however, if one goes
at a quiet time, in the words of a recent pilgrim, 'it is
peaceful, spacious and overpoweringly holy'. This is
a fascinating and extraordinary place, which may
challenge our Western preconceptions, but it does
have an evocative and eccentric charm and
atmosphere. It is richly, and one may think rather
haphazardly adorned: a contradiction of rich hanging
brocades, festoons of (by now familiar!) dusty
devotional hanging oil lamps, an unusual painted, stiff
leather lining to the long narrow, marble-floored
cavern facing the small apse, and again, the smoke
grime from centuries of lamps burning in silent
prayer. There are also some rather inelegant
industrial-looking mesh grilles, no doubt protecting
precious items on the altars, all lit by bright, bare
electric light bulbs.

The focal point is a small apse containing the Altar
of Christ's Birth, under which is a large, silver
fourteen-pointed star inlaid over the marble floor. The
star bears the inscription, *'Hic de Virgine Maria Jesus*

Christus natus est 1717'. It is here that pilgrims kneel, touch or kiss the star, remembering in prayer and veneration the infant King born here in such humble surroundings. There are two other smaller, facing altars, at a lower level than the Grotto altar, variously described as the Altar of the Manger and the Altar of the Magi.

The Nativity

"So Joseph set out from the town of Nazareth in Galilee for Judaea, to David's town called Bethlehem, since he was of David's House and line, in order to be registered together with Mary, his betrothed, who was with child. Now it happened that, while they were there, the time came for her to have her child, and she gave birth to a son, her first born. She wrapped him in swaddling clothes and laid him in a manger because there was no room for them in the living space". (*Lk* 2:4-7).

Meditation

[Jesus speaks:] "I was born, born for you, in a cave, in December, in the cold, homeless, in the middle of a winter's night, in the unheard-of poverty of the extremely poor, in solitude, in an abandonment unique in this world. What, my children, do I want you to learn from my birth? To believe in my love, to believe that I have loved you until now. To hope in me, who have loved you so dearly. I want to teach you to despise the ways of the world, which was so unimportant to me. I want to teach you poverty, lowliness, solitude, humility, penance. I want to teach you to love me, for I was not content with giving myself to the world in the Incarnation, sanctifying it invisibly in the visitation; no, that did not satisfy my love. From the moment of my birth onward, I showed myself to you, giving myself wholly to you, putting myself in your hands. From then on, you could touch me, hear me, possess me, serve me, console me. Love me now; I am so close to you." (*Blessed Charles de Foucaud*)

Canticle

"Let us give thanks to the Father
for having made you worthy
to share the lot of the saints in light.

He rescued us from the power of darkness
and brought us
into the kingdom of his beloved Son.
Through him we have redemption,
the forgiveness of our sins.

He is the image of the invisible God,
the first-born of all creatures.
In him everything in heaven
and on earth was created,
things visible and invisible". (*Col* 1:12-16)

Here, also may be prayed the Third Joyful Mystery
of the Rosary - The Birth of Jesus.

SAINTS

Church of St Catherine

Exit from the Grotto is by the stairs opposite, into
the north transept chapel, owned by the Armenians,
the altar to the right being dedicated to the Three
Kings, the one ahead to Our Lady. One can exit this
chapel into the adjacent Roman Catholic church of
St Catherine.

This relatively modern church (enlarged in 1881),
dedicated to St Catherine of Alexandria, gives stark
contrast to the ancient Basilica and Grotto next door.
It is a light, airy church, pillared, arched and bare
stoned. Above the sanctuary there is a dramatic star-
shaped amber glass window with its rays
surrounding a square picture of Mary, Joseph and
Franciscans adoring Jesus. Note the dramatic

catherine-wheel lights denoting the instrument of torture under which St Catherine suffered, finally being beheaded in c. 305, a virgin martyr, for her faith. If one needs some peace, quiet and space to rest, pray, meditate and reflect on your experience in the Holy Grotto, there is a small, separate Blessed Sacrament side chapel - and here one can marvel at the sublime gift of Jesus in the Eucharist, present with us now, just that very short distance from the place where God became Man.

St Jerome

From the church one can descend into another complex of caves, all beautifully restored by the Franciscans in 1964, tastefully presented and subtly lit. Firstly, there is the Chapel of the Innocents, commemorating Herod's attempt to kill the new born Jesus, then a Chapel dedicated to St Joseph; to the right, the double cave of St Jerome, the first with his former tomb, the second where it is said he translated the Bible. It is back-to-basics bare rock, such a contrast to the Grotto of the Nativity, to which these caves are linked. I was moved when listening to two separate groups of pilgrims worshipping in the two chapels, hearing the evocative and heartfelt singing.

Exiting from the back doors of St Catherine's takes you into a small, tranquil pillared and arched cloister, overlooked from above by a statue of Our Lady, but in the centre of which, fittingly, stands St Jerome.

St George

Leaving the cloisters through the entrance lobby into Manger Square, you come across a life-sized, action packed statue of St George in full armour, on a plunging horse, cape flying, lance being thrust into the dragon. I could not help but notice his rather neat moustache and slightly disdainful expression as he went about his business of slaying the dragon! St George is the most unlikely of patron saints of England, as his origins are quite obscure, and far from England. According to the apocryphal Acts of St George, as told in the Eastern Church from the fifth century, George was a tribune in the Roman army who was beheaded by Diocletian for protesting against the Emperor's persecution of Christians. He rapidly became venerated throughout Christendom as an example of bravery in defence of the poor and the defenceless and of the Christian faith. He started to become known in the West, and in England, from returning Crusaders who told of this Roman tribune who was martyred for his faith.

He was adopted as a patron saint of soldiers after he was said to have appeared to the Crusader army at the battle of Antioch in 1098. When Richard I was campaigning in Palestine he put his army under the protection of St George. He was acknowledged as patron saint of England by the end of the 14th century, and in 1415, the year of Agincourt, Archbishop Chichele declared St George's Day to be a great feast and ordered it to be observed like Christmas Day. The red cross of the martyr against a white background proclaims his distinctive identity, as well as all the trappings of chivalry (Knights of the Garter) and bravery (George Cross), that go with it. St George features quite regularly in the Holy Land, and is widely venerated in the Eastern churches - keep an eye out for him!

Prayer to St George

Faithful servant of God
and invincible martyr, St George,
inflamed with an ardent love of Christ,
you fought against the dragon of pride,
falsehood and deceit.
Neither pain nor torture, nor the sword
nor death could part you from the love of Christ.

I implore you for the sake of this love
to help me by your intercession
to overcome the temptations
that surround me,
and to bear bravely the trials that oppress me
so that I may patiently carry my cross
and let neither distress nor difficulty
separate me from the love
of Our Lord Jesus Christ. Amen.
(*CTS prayer card*)

SHEPHERDS' FIELDS

Just over two kilometres from Manger Square, still within the Palestinian Authority area of Bethlehem, in the village of Beit Sahour, lie the Shepherds' Fields, which commemorate the angelic announcement to the shepherds and the world of the birth of the Son of God. The precise location is not known, but certainly at the time of Jesus' birth, these open fields below the town are where the shepherds would have been, looking after their flocks and settling down for the night in one of the many caves in this area. There is also a Greek Orthodox site close by, with its distinctive modern, red-domed church, which also commemorates this event.

The area, known as the Shepherds' Fields, is run by the Franciscans and is in a spacious, pleasant garden setting, an ideal place to seek some peace and quiet. Although the site offers fine shimmering views across the hardy landscape, the nearby encroaching suburbs of Bethlehem have to be 'filtered out', as do the visible and jarring outskirts of Jerusalem in the distance. Within the grounds there are the ruins of a Byzantine agricultural monastery, with remains of winepresses, a bakery, querns, cisterns and animal pens. The apse of the monastery church also survives, and a large lintel, embellished with crosses. There are some smoke blackened caves, of which one of the larger ones has been turned into a small rudimentary chapel.

Chapel of the Angels

Crowning the whole site though, is the striking and modern (1953), Barluzzi church, the Chapel of the Angels, designed in the style of a nomadic tent. The pale, smooth, canted stonework at each corner supports the contrasting, rougher bricks of the 'tent' walls. The whole supports a graceful, arched bell gable, and is topped by a gleaming white cupola studded with circular glass inlets, allowing light to pour into the interior. Above the simple, oblong entrance door hovers a bronze angel in silent proclamation. It is circular inside, four figures support the central altar, which is surrounded by three side apses, each of which show beautiful frescoes of the Nativity, the Angelic announcement to the shepherds, and the shepherds joyfully making their way to Bethlehem.

Angelic announcement

"In the countryside close by there were shepherds out in the fields keeping guard over their sheep during the watches of the night. An angel of the Lord stood over them and the glory of the Lord shone round them. They were terrified, but the angel said, 'Do not be afraid. Look, I bring you news of great joy, a joy to be shared by the whole people. Today in the town of David a Saviour has been born to you; he is Christ the Lord. And here is a sign for you: you will find a baby wrapped in swaddling clothes and lying in a manger. And all at once with the angel there was a great throng of the hosts of heaven, praising God with the words:

Glory to God in the highest heaven, and on earth peace for those he favours". (*Lk* 2:8-11)

Meditation

O night of admiration, full of choirs,
O night of deepest praise,
And darkness full of sweet delight!
What secret and intrepid Visitor
Has come to raise us from the dead?
He softly springs the locks of time, our sepulchre,
In the foretold encounter. (*Fr Thomas Merton*)

After Bethlehem - the hidden life

*"During the greater part of his life Jesus shared the
condition of the vast majority of human beings; a
daily life spent without evident greatness, a life of
manual labour. His religious life was that of a Jew
obedient to the law of God, a life in the community.
From this whole period it is revealed to us that Jesus
was 'obedient' to his parents, and that, "His mother
stored up all these things in her heart. And Jesus
increased in wisdom, in stature, and in favour with
God and with people". (Lk 2:51, 52) (CCC 531).*

And it was from this life 'without evident
greatness' that Jesus set out from Nazareth, aged
about thirty, to meet his cousin John the Baptist at the
River Jordan, to be baptised, signalling the start of His
public ministry, as described in the next Chapter.

❧ THE ROAD ❧ TO MINISTRY

❦ BAPTISM ❦

"It was at this time that Jesus came from Nazareth in Galilee and was baptised in the Jordan by John." (*Mk* 1:9)

"Jesus' public life starts with His baptism by John in the River Jordan. It was, "on his part the acceptance and inauguration of his mission as God's suffering Servant. He allows himself to be numbered among sinners; he is already 'the Lamb of God who takes away the sins of the world'. Already he is anticipating the 'baptism' of his bloody death. Already he is coming to 'fulfil all righteousness', that is, he is submitting himself entirely to His Father's will: out of love he consents to this baptism of death for the remission of our sins" (*CCC* 536).

River Jordan

The ancient site commemorating the Baptism of Jesus is in a restricted military zone, north of the Dead Sea, and is open to the public only once a year. Today, pilgrims recall Christ's baptism at another site, just south of the Sea of Galilee, where the Jordan empties into it, and not far from the lakeside town of Tiberias. Here is the

River Jordan - baptismal site.

extensive, developed site of Yardenit, built by an enterprising Israeli commune, where pilgrims generally head to commemorate this event. It is well spread and laid out, with custom-built baptismal pools at the riverside, allowing easy and safe access into the river, and good vantage points over the river. There is a well stocked shop, selling a wide range of devotional and local goods, a snack bar, toilets and changing rooms for those who are undergoing full immersion baptism.

But despite all this, it is sympathetically set in this tranquil spot by the shady, tree-lined river, quite wide at this point, as it flows gently past. This of course is an ideal place to renew one's baptismal vows, either publicly as a group, or individually. It is also the opportunity to take some Jordan water home with you to keep for family or other special baptismal occasions. Whilst it can be busy, and there may be some exuberance, as some groups face the joyful prospect of baptism, one can find the odd quiet spot and reflect at this starting point of Jesus' public ministry.

Meditation

Baptism is God's most beautiful and magnificent gift... We call it gift, grace, anointing, enlightenment, garment of immortality, bath of rebirth, seal and most precious gift. It is called gift because it is

conferred on those who bring nothing of their own; grace since it is given to the guilty; Baptism because sin is buried in the water, anointing for it is priestly and royal as those who are anointed; enlightenment because it radiates light; clothing since it veils our shame; bath because it washes; and seal as it is our guard and the sign of God's Lordship.
(*St Gregory of Nazianzus*)

Prayer of Baptismal Renewal

Through the tender mercy of the Eternal Father I have been given God's most beautiful gift of Baptism in the name of Our Lord Jesus. With it I was clothed with the garment of immortality which I now seek to wash through with Your cleansing and living waters. By this renewal I seek Your holy re-anointing, further enlightenment, and a re-sealing of my covenant with You. In Your presence, and that of Your beloved Son who was baptised in these waters, I call down Your Holy Spirit of Love to bless and sanctify this act of renewal:

Once again, I renounce Satan, all his works, all his temptations.

I restate my firm belief in God, the Father Almighty, Creator of heaven and earth; in Jesus

Christ, his only Son, our Lord, who was born into this world and who suffered and died for my sins and rose again; in the Holy Spirit, the Holy Catholic Church, the communion of Saints, the forgiveness of sins, the resurrection of the body and life everlasting.

Having been buried with Christ unto death and raised up with him unto a new life, I pledge to live no longer for self or selfish world, but for Him who died for my sins and rose again to set me free, to continue serving God, my heavenly Father, faithfully and unto death, in the holy Catholic Church, and to listen to, and trust in the guidance of His Holy Spirit.

Taught by our Saviour's command and formed by the word of God, I now have the courage to say: Our Father, who art in heaven...

I saw water flowing
from the right side of the temple, alleluia,
It brought God's life and his salvation,
and the people sang in joyful praise:
alleluia, alleluia. (cf *Ez*:1-2,9)

"And when Jesus had been baptised he at once came up from the water, and suddenly the heavens

opened and he saw the Spirit of God descending like a dove and coming down on him. And suddenly there was a voice from heaven, 'This is my Son, the Beloved; my favour rests on him.'" (*Mt* 3:16,17).

The First Mystery of Light can be prayed here: The Baptism of Jesus in the River Jordan.

❧ TEMPTATION ❧

"Then Jesus was led by the Spirit out into the desert to be put to the test by the devil." (Mt 4:1)

"Jesus' temptation reveals the way in which the Son of God is Messiah, contrary to the way Satan proposes to him and the way men wish to attribute to him. This is why Christ vanquished the Tempter for us: for we have not a high priest who is unable to sympathise with our weaknesses, but one who in every respect has been tested as we are, yet without sinning. By the solemn forty days of Lent the Church unites herself each year to the mystery of Jesus in the desert." (CCC 540).

Temptation Sites

Jesus' Temptation is described in the Gospels as having taken place in three different locations: 'the desert', 'the holy city' (Jerusalem), and 'a high mountain'. There is of course plenty of 'desert' (the Judean desert) between the drive from Jericho, the place of the high mountain, to Jerusalem and the Temple. Where you visit, or where you stop to pray and meditate over Jesus' Temptation, will depend on circumstance, opportunity, and your own preference.

Depending on the local security situation, it is not always possible to visit Jericho, but by driving through the town to the far end one can look up at the 5th century Greek monastery (St George's) which clings to the rock face of the Mount of Temptation - the 'Mountain of the Forty Days'. Its protective wall is visible, together with hermits' caves. Men only are allowed to climb the steep track and visit the monks, but this requires an entire day. Driving on to Jerusalem one should be able to select a suitable vantage point en route to look out over a piece of desert wilderness and meditate. And in Jerusalem the Temple of the Mount, on what is now an important Islamic site, is open to visitors, as is the Western Wall at the foot of the Temple. Discretion will be required if praying at these locations.

The Temptation of Jesus

"Then Jesus was led by the Spirit out into the desert to be put to the test by the devil. He fasted for forty days and forty nights, after which he was hungry, and the tester came and said to him, 'If you are Son of God, tell these stones to turn into loaves.' But he replied, 'Scripture says: 'Human beings live not on bread alone but on every word that comes from the mouth of God.' The devil then took him to the holy city and set him on the parapet of the Temple. 'If you are Son of God,' he said, 'throw yourself down, for

Scripture says: 'He has given his angels orders about you, and they will carry you in their arms in case you trip over a stone.' Jesus said to him, Scripture also says: 'Do not put the Lord your God to the test.' Next taking him to a very high mountain, the devil showed him all the kingdoms of the world and their splendour. And he said to him, 'I will give you all these if you fall at my feet and do me homage.' Then Jesus replied, 'Away with you, Satan! For Scripture says: 'The Lord your God is the one to whom you must do homage, him alone you must serve.' Then the devil left him, and suddenly angels appeared and looked after him". (Mt 4:1-11)

Meditation

The whole diabolic temptation took place from without, not from within. If we look at the progress of his temptation, we see how great the struggle was that set us free from temptation. Our ancient enemy rose up against the first human being, our ancestor in three temptations. He tempted him by gluttony, by vainglory, and by avarice. And he overcame him when he tempted him, because he subjugated him through consent. He tempted him by gluttony when he showed him the forbidden food of the tree, and told him: 'Taste it.' He tempted him by vainglory when he said, 'You will be like gods.' He tempted him by adding avarice when he said, 'knowing good and evil.' Avarice is concerned not only with money but also with high position. We rightly call it avarice when we seek high position beyond measure. If grasping at honour was not related to avarice, Paul would not have said of God's only-begotten Son: 'He did not think that being equal to God was something to be grasped.' The devil drew our ancestor to pride by stirring him up to an avaricious desire for high position.

But the means by which he overcame the first man were the same ones which caused him to yield when he tempted the second. He tempted him by gluttony when he said, 'Tell these stones to become bread.' He tempted him by vainglory when he said, 'If you are Son of God cast yourself down.' He tempted him by an avaricious desire for high position when he showed him all the kingdoms of the world, saying, 'I will give you all these if you will fall down and worship me.' The second man overcame him by the same means he had boasted that he used to overcome the first man. As a captive he would depart from our hearts by the same avenue which had given him entrance when he possessed us. (*St Gregory the Great*)

❧ DIVINITY ❧

"On the third day there was a wedding at Cana in Galilee." (*Jn* 2:1)

"On the threshold of his public life Jesus performs his first sign, at his mother's request, during a wedding feast. The Church attaches great importance to Jesus' presence at the wedding at Cana. She sees in it the confirmation of the goodness of marriage and the proclamation that thenceforth marriage will be an efficacious sign of Christ's presence" (*CCC* 1613).

Cana

Five miles north of Nazareth is the small, rather dozy town of Cana, *Kafr Kanna*, with its simple flat-roofed, whitewashed houses. Here, Jesus, at the beginning of His ministry, revealed His divinity through the miracle of turning the water into wine at the wedding feast at which, "the mother of Jesus was there, and Jesus and His disciples had also been invited" (*Jn* 2:2). In corroborating tradition, St Paula and St Eustochium, disciples of St Jerome in Bethlehem, wrote in the fourth century in a letter that they, 'saw Cana, not far from Nazareth, where the water was changed into wine'.

CHURCH OF THE WEDDING FEAST

The event is commemorated by the Franciscan Church of the Wedding Feast, built in 1879, over the remains of the previous Byzantine and Crusader buildings evident below, in the crypt. It is a small church, sitting quietly at the back of a diminutive, sunny square. It has a stolid symmetry: twin bell towers and red dome, fronted by an upper balcony and a well proportioned, arcaded narthex. Inside, you will see a plain, unadorned bare-stoned church, with a single aisle, no windows, and a domed sanctuary. It is built on two levels, with the upper level preserving the remains of the crypt underneath.

In the floor near the entrance to the crypt, under a metal grill, is an Aramaic inscription from the third century, 'Honoured be the memory of Josef, son of Tanham, son of Buta and his sons who made this [bench], may it be a blessing to them. Amen.' The tradition is that Yosef may have been Joseph of Tiberias, who converted to Christianity during the Constantinian period, building many churches in Galilee. In the crypt is a commemorative water pot, symbolic of what this church stands for: also to be seen are the remains of an ancient water cistern and other vessels of varying antiquity.

The wedding at Cana

"On the third day there was a wedding at Cana in Galilee. The mother of Jesus was there, and Jesus and his disciples had also been invited. And they ran out of wine, since the wine provided for the feast had all been used, and the mother of Jesus said to him, 'They have no wine.' Jesus said, 'Woman, what do you want from me? My hour has not come yet.' His mother said to the servants, 'Do whatever he tells you.' There were six stone water jars standing there, meant for the ablutions that are customary among the Jews: each could hold twenty or thirty gallons. Jesus said to the servants, 'Fill the jars with water,' and they filled them to the brim. Then he said to them, 'Draw some out now and take it to the president of the feast.' They did this; the president tasted the water, and it had turned into wine. Having no idea where it came from - though the servants who had drawn the water knew - the president of the feast called the bridegroom and said, 'Everyone serves good wine first, and the worst wine when the guests are well wined, but you have kept the best wine till now'. This was the first of Jesus' signs: it was at Cana in Galilee. He revealed his glory, and his disciples believed in him." (Jn 2:1-11)

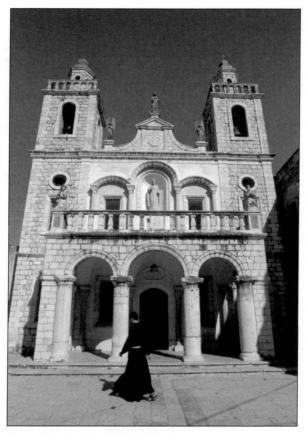

Cana - Church of the Wedding Feast.

Renewal of marriage vows

(In a group situation your Spiritual Director may wish to conduct a public liturgy. The following is designed for a private renewal of vows.)

Father, how can we ever express the blessings of our marriage, joined by the Church, strengthened by an offering, sealed by a blessing, announced by angels, witnessed by our faith community and ratified by the Father? How wonderful this bond between two believers, now one in hope, one in desire, one in discipline, one in the same service! We are both children of one Father and servants of the same Master, undivided in spirit and flesh, truly two in one flesh. Where our flesh is one, there is also one spirit. (cf Tertullian, *ad uxorem*)

Father, on this day, and at this place, we give thanks for the holy union in which you have gifted us and enjoined us. As we look back, we give thanks for the joys and sorrows, the tears and laughter, the gifts and graces, the trials and tribulations. We now look forward to more giving, less taking; more love, more laughter; more commitment, more caring. In recognising our human weakness we pray for inspiration from the exemplary union of Mary and

Joseph, to strengthen us and prepare us for our continuing journey ahead. We ask you to continue blessing and sanctifying us in this sacred sacrament, and we pledge our loyalty and love once again to each other, and to You, being bound securely with Your saving love. Amen.

Meditation

This lovely reading from St Paul that follows, about love, is often put in the context of marriage. Fearful of your being too familiar with it, please contemplate and meditate it slowly and sweetly with new eyes and open hearts:

"Set your mind on the higher gifts. And now I am going to put before you the best way of all. Though I command languages both human and angelic - if I speak without love, I am no more than a gong booming or a cymbal clashing. And though I have the power of prophecy, to penetrate all mysteries and knowledge, and though I have all the faith necessary to move mountains - if I am without love, I am nothing. Though I should give away to the poor all that I possess, and even give up my body to be burned - if I am without love, it will do me no good whatever.

Love is always patient and kind; love is never jealous; love is not boastful or conceited, it is never rude and never seeks its own advantage, it does not take offence or store up grievances. Love does not rejoice at wrongdoing, but finds its joy in the truth. It is always ready to make allowances, to trust, to hope and endure whatever comes. Love never comes to an end." (1 *Co* 12:31-13:8)

The Second Mystery of Light can be prayed here: Jesus Reveals His Divinity at the Wedding of Cana.

Close by is a Greek Orthodox church celebrating the same event. Opposite the church is a local shop, selling, amongst the usual devotional items, traditional Cana wine, which I found extremely sweet and sticky!

Preparation for Ministry

"This was the first of Jesus' signs: it was at Cana in Galilee. He revealed his glory and his disciples believed in him." (Jn 1:11)

This first miracle, or sign, was the precursor to the many miracles that Jesus would perform during his ministry, which initially took root in Capernaum, on the Sea of Galilee, which is where we travel next.

MINISTRY IN GALILEE

☞ GALILEE AND CAPERNAUM ☜

"....he withdrew to Galilee, and leaving Nazara he went and settled in Capernaum, beside the lake..." (Mt 4:13)

"Now after John was arrested, Jesus came into Galilee, preaching the gospel of God, and saying: "The time is fulfilled, and the kingdom of God is at hand: repent and believe in the gospel."' 'To carry out the will of the Father, Christ inaugurated the kingdom of heaven on earth.' Now the Father's will is 'to raise up people to share in his own divine life'. He does this by gathering them around his Son Jesus Christ. This gathering is the Church, 'on earth the seed and beginning of that kingdom'." (CCC 541)

Lake Galilee

A great deal of Jesus' ministry was conducted in the Galilee area, much of it based at Capernaum, which, in His day was a thriving fishing town on the northern end of the Sea of Galilee, but is now the scene of archaeological ruins. What is certain is that the largely unspoilt scenery and tranquil atmosphere around the Sea of Galilee is on the whole unchanged since Jesus'

Sea of Galilee.

time - in fact there is every indication that it could be quieter now than it was then, as there is evidence that the northern end of the Lake was a busy place, with a thriving fishing and olive industry. It lay astride the busy east-west trade routes from Egypt into Syria, and was probably one reason why Jesus chose to live and work from there.

The teardrop shaped Sea of Galilee is part of the extensive geological Rift Valley fault-line reaching all the way northwards from Africa. The Sea is about 200 metres below the level of the Mediterranean, is twenty-one kilometres long and twelve wide, and some fifty metres at its deepest. Unlike its counterpart further south, the Dead Sea, Galilee is in the so called 'Mediterranean zone'. It is very much alive, with an abundance of marine life, flora and fauna. Surrounded by fertile hills, in springtime the region is green and lush, bursting with life and vitality.

Confusingly it has several names: being landlocked, of fresh water and not too large, 'Lake' would seem an obvious label, but it is also referred to as 'Sea'. Certainly when one witnesses the fierce storms that whip up and funnel through from the surrounding hills, as recounted by Mark: "Then it began to blow a great gale, and the waves were breaking into the boat so it was almost swamped..." (*Mk* 4:37), one can see that it assumes some very 'sea-like' characteristics! It is also referred to by John as the Sea of Tiberias, after the large town on its western edge, and by Luke as Lake Gennesaret, referring to the Gentile's territory on its eastern shore. Today, you may see signs pointing to Lake Kinnereth, the Hebrew for harp, after its shape.

Peter's boat and Peter's fish

In 1986 two brothers saw the shape of a sunken boat in the unusually lowered water levels of the Sea of Galilee. The subsequent recovery of this boat revealed a 26.5 foot long vessel very similar in description to those fishing boats used in Jesus' time. Archaeological assessment and isotopic testing confirmed that this boat was of that era. The 'Kinneret Boat' is on view at Kibbutz Ginossar on the Sea of Galilee.

The other 'step-back' in time that the pilgrim can make is to partake of the bony but tasty 'Peter's Fish' offered in Galilean restaurants. Fished in the Sea of Galilee, it is so called because of the distinctive (Peter's) 'thumbprint' on the fishes' sides.

CAPERNAUM

That Capernaum (Hebrew *Kefar Nahum*) is a significant place in Jesus' ministry is very evident from the Gospels. He lived here with Peter and his family, healing Peter's mother-in-law (*Mt* 8:14-17).

He preached extensively in the synagogue close to Peter's house (*Mk* 1:21), worked many miracles, amongst which was the healing of the centurion's servant (*Mt* 8:5-13), raising Jairus' daughter from the dead (*Mt* 9:18-26), healing the great multitudes brought to Him (*Mt* 8:16-17; 9:36-38). From here he also gathered some of His Apostles, the 'fishers of men', among them Peter and Andrew, James and John (*Mk* 1:16-20). Matthew the customs officer extracting taxes from the fishermen and passing caravans on the trade route, also came from here, "...he saw a man named Matthew sitting at the tax office, and he said to him, 'Follow me.' And he got up and followed him" (*Mt* 9:9), and John, James and Philip came from nearby Bethsaida.

But in spite of His preaching and presence there, and the many miracles performed as His witness, the inhabitants were not convinced or converted in any large number. This provoked Jesus' bitter rebuke, "And as for you Capernaum, did you want to be raised as high as heaven? You shall be flung down to hell. For if the miracles done in you had been done in Sodom, it would have been standing yet. Still I tell you that it will be more bearable for Sodom on Judgement Day than for you" (*Mt* 11:23-24). Today's mute ruins bear witness to that lament over this lakeside town.

Capernaum's treasures

Since Jesus' time, and after the First and Second Jewish Revolts, the Galilean area was settled by Jews fleeing from Jerusalem, particularly to nearby Tiberias, which became the home of refugee rabbis, and eventually the birthplace of the Talmud, the Jewish commentary on the Scriptures. There were a number of early Christian settlements in Galilee, but after the fall of Byzantine rule, the area was increasingly occupied by Muslims in 8/9th centuries, and later by Turcoman tribes from central Asia, and by Druze.

Unlike Tiberias, which continued to thrive, Capernaum fell into disuse over a thousand years ago, and it was only in the late 19th century that scholars started to take more interest in the area, with the Franciscans purchasing part of the site. Some selective excavations in the early 20th century revealed the remains of a 4th century synagogue and a 5th century octagonal church. Amazingly, it was not until 1968 that more extensive excavations brought to light, and made sense of the full treasures of Capernaum.

THE HOUSE OF PETER

Although previous excavations revealed the 5th century octagonal church and the 4th century synagogue, what emerged after subsequent investigation was the 'House of Peter' under the octagonal church. Archaeologists claim that the house existed before Jesus' time, and the evidence points to it being used in the late 1st century as a *Domus Ecclesia* or *titulus* (house church) by the early Judeo Christians. Its constant use as such is supported by the fact that the walls were re-plastered on a number of occasions, the floor re-laid with lime. Over a hundred inscriptions in Aramaic, Greek and Hebrew were discovered, saying 'Jesus', 'Lord', 'Christ' several times and 'Peter' twice.

This was the house church visited by Egeria in the 4th century, "Moreover, in Capernaum the house of the Prince of the Apostles has been made into a church, with its original walls still standing. It is where the Lord healed the paralytic" (*Mk* 2:1-12). Late in the 5th century an octagonal church with ambulatory and a mosaic floor was built in the martyrion tradition of Jerusalem, faithfully following the outlines of the original *Domus Eclesia*. This church was destroyed around 636 during the Muslim conquest, and along with the rest of Capernaum over the next centuries, slipped quietly into obscurity and ruin.

Synagogue

The remains of the 4th century synagogue are striking and substantial. It is built in a handsome pale limestone in contrast to the dark basalt volcanic rock

Capernaum - 4th century synagogue.

native to the area, of which other buildings are constructed. The clue to this synagogue being built alongside the original 1st century synagogue, in which Jesus preached, is its original foundations of black basalt, clearly seen as you climb the steps into the main prayer hall. And in Egeria's words, "There is also the synagogue where the Lord cured a man possessed by the devil (*Mk* 1:23). The way in is up many stairs, and it is made of dressed stone."

Although completely open to the skies the main prayer hall displays many pillars, with a main aisle and two small side aisles, which probably supported an upper gallery running round three sides, possibly as the women's prayer and observation area. The stonework is richly decorated with symbols such as the *menorah* (candelabrum) adorning a Corinthian style capital, and others featuring fruits and palms and geometric designs, including the Star of David.

Next to the prayer hall is a courtyard, which was enclosed on three sides by colonnaded cloisters. Surrounding the synagogue are the excavated remains of the simple family houses of the 1st century. You will see that many follow the pattern of the windowed rooms facing inwards onto what was the family courtyard, where the occupants no doubt socialised, ate and slept.

Today's church

However, what is most striking about today's site is the modern (1990) octagonal church rather dramatically suspended by slender pillars over the original church and Peter's House. What came to my mind when I first saw it, was a clam shell, with its flat, thin structure, many jaw-like windows round the sides, and soft external curves top and bottom. It is just as striking inside, combining simplicity (lack of clutter and its airiness) with elegance, by its tiered seats, glass bottomed floor looking down on Peter's House, and stunning views out across the Sea of Galilee.

This is a lovely site to wander round. It is well presented and spacious, with an abundance of palm and eucalyptus trees, bougainvillaea and other greenery. There are many interesting artefacts also on display round the site: carved limestone items, including a relief depicting the Ark of the Covenant on wheels, a Roman milestone from the ancient *via Maris* trade route, mosaics, and olive presses in the local black basalt. There is also an enormous millstone, bringing to mind Jesus' words "...anyone who is the downfall of one of these little ones who have faith in me, it would be better drowned into the depths of the sea with a great millstone round his neck" (*Mt* 18:5-6). It is also interesting to ponder over the juxtaposition of the synagogue where Jesus

preached and the subsequent growth and position of
the Christian church just next door, and from this
quiet seaside town, to the churches round the world.

Meditation

Prayer to Jesus is answered by him already during
his ministry, through signs that anticipate the
power of his death and Resurrection: Jesus hears
the prayer of faith, expressed in words (the leper,
Jairus, the Canaanite woman, the good thief) or in
silence (the bearers of the paralytic, the woman
with a haemorrhage who touches his clothes, the
tears and ointment of the sinful woman). The
urgent request of the blind men, 'Have mercy on
us, Son of David' or, 'Jesus, Son of David, have
mercy on me!', has been renewed in the traditional
prayer to Jesus known as the Jesus Prayer: 'Lord
Jesus Christ, Son of God, have mercy on me, a
sinner!' Healing infirmities or forgiving sins, Jesus
always responds to a prayer offered in faith: 'Your
faith has made you well, go in peace.' St Augustine
wonderfully summarises the three dimensions of
Jesus' prayer: 'He prays for us as our priest, prays
in us as our Head, and is prayed to, by us, as our
God. Therefore let us acknowledge our voice in
him and his in us'. (*CCC* 2616)

Prayer

Taken from the meditation above is this deceptively simple and repetitive, meditative prayer. It holds great depths and abundant riches; ponder it deeply as you slowly turn it over, and indeed expand on it, in your mind and your heart:

"Lord Jesus Christ, Son of God, have mercy on me, a sinner!"

Here are some thoughts:

Lord.... we acknowledge and hail you as Lord and Master, but we know you are the Lord who came not to master, but to serve, to feed; a caring shepherd to lead his sheep, a humble servant to wash our feet, an innocent Lamb to willingly die for us.

Jesus.... means 'God saves', the Divine instrument made human to lift the burden of sin from mankind, to lead us to the Eternal Jerusalem.

Christ.... the Messiah, the Saviour, the one consecrated by God and anointed by the Holy Spirit as priest, prophet and king, 'who gives his life as the ransom for the many' (*Mt* 20:28).

Son of God.... the Second Person of the Holy Trinity, the only Son of the Father, born through the love of the Holy Spirit to proclaim the Word of God, to display the image of the Father on Earth. By his perfect example as a human person He came to give hope and inspiration to humankind; to come closer to us through His own humanity.

have mercy.... as he showed to the adulterous woman, 'Neither do I condemn you,' (*Jn* 8:11); as he did on the Cross to the Penitent Sinner, 'In truth, I tell you today you will be with me in paradise' (*Lk* 23:43). As God the Father has mercy on all those who repent, no matter how dark their sin, for, when 'we were dead in our sins,' He 'brought us to life with Christ.' (*Eph* 2:5).

on me.... an individual, not just a faceless one amongst the mass, about whom God assures each one of us that, 'I will not forget you. Look, I have engraved you in the palms of my hands,' (*Is* 49:16), 'You created my inmost self, / knit me together in my mother's womb.' (*Ps* 139:13).

a sinner.... we are all sinners, but, Jesus invites all sinners to the table of the kingdom: 'I came not to call the righteous, but sinners.' (*Mk* 2:17); but to eat at that table we must be open to God's will and constantly endeavour for that conversion 'without which one cannot enter the kingdom.' (cf *CCC* 545). (*David Baldwin*)

❧ BEATITUDES ❧

"How blessed are the poor in spirit: the Kingdom of Heaven is theirs." (*Mt* 5:3)

"The Beatitudes are at the heart of Jesus' preaching...[They] depict the countenance of Jesus Christ and portray his charity. They express the vocation of the faithful associated with the glory of his Passion and Resurrection; they shed light on the actions and attitudes characteristic of the Christian life; they are the paradoxical promises that sustain hope in the midst of tribulations; they proclaim the blessings and rewards already secured, however dimly, for Christ's disciples; they have begun in the lives of the Virgin Mary and all the saints." (*CCC* 1716, 1717)

CHURCH OF THE BEATITUDES

For once, in this turbulent land, we can visit a chapel built where there were no former buildings, occupations or known 'history'. This is the Church of the Beatitudes built on land acquired by the National Association for Aid to Italian Missionaries in 1926, with the church designed by Barluzzi, being completed in 1938. It commemorates Jesus' famous discourse recorded in Chapters 5 - 7 of Matthew's Gospel, which starts with the eight Beatitudes. Whilst there is no specific mention of the exact location where Jesus preached this sermon - the Sermon on the Mount - it is likely to have been on the northern shores of Lake Galilee on a hillside near Capernaum, overlooking the lake, such as the setting for this church.

This beautiful, tranquil setting is perfectly fitted to this simple but striking church. It is octagonal in shape and is encompassed by a colonnaded veranda of contrasting white arches and delicate pillars. The central dome is crowned by a small, pillared lantern, and a bell gable sits back from the main arched entrance. Inside, the altar is centrally placed, and above it is an elegant arch of contrasting alabaster and onyx curves. The dome is a plain glittering gold mosaic, beneath which sit eight windows bearing the opening texts of Jesus' Beatitudes. The narrow horizontal windows at the lower level afford fine views of the surrounding area. The striking floor mosaic represents the seven petitions made in the Lord's Prayer (*Mt* 6:9-13).

This was one of the places that Pope John Paul II visited in March 2000, at which he celebrated Mass for young people. In his sermon he told them:

"In the end, Jesus does not merely speak the Beatitudes. He lives the Beatitudes. *He is the*

Church of the Beatitudes.

Beatitudes. Looking at him you will see what it means to be poor in spirit, gentle and merciful, to mourn, to care for what is right, to be pure in heart, to make peace, to be persecuted. This is why Jesus has the right to say, 'Come, follow me!' He does not say simply, 'Do what I say'. He says, 'Come, follow me!'"

There are quite extensive, well kept gardens outside; with its commanding views, and its peaceful location, it is the perfect place to meditate deeply on those most profound sayings of Jesus.

The Beatitudes

"How blessed are the poor in spirit:
the kingdom of Heaven is theirs.
Blessed are the gentle:
they shall have
the earth as inheritance.
Blessed are those who mourn:
they shall be comforted.
Blessed are those who hunger and
thirst for righteousness:
they shall have their fill.
Blessed are the merciful:
they shall have mercy shown them.
Blessed are the pure in heart:
they shall see God.

Blessed are the peacemakers:
they shall be recognised
as children of God.
Blessed are those who are persecuted
in the cause of righteousness:
the kingdom of Heaven is theirs.

Blessed are you when people abuse you and persecute you and speak all kinds of calumny against you falsely on my account. Rejoice and be glad, for your reward will be great in heaven; this is how they persecuted the prophets before you". (*Mt* 5:3-12)

Meditation

I say to you: Blessed is he who exposes himself to an existence never brought under mastery, who does not transcend but, rather, abandons himself to my ever-transcending grace. Blessed are not the enlightened whose every question has been answered and who are delighted with their own sublime light, the mature and ripe ones whose one remaining action is to fall from the tree: blessed, rather, are the chased, the harassed who must daily stand before my enigmas and cannot solve them. Blessed are the poor in spirit, those who lack a spirit of cleverness. Woe to the rich, and woe doubly to the rich in spirit! Although nothing is impossible with God, it is difficult for the Spirit to move their fat heart. The poor are willing and easy to direct. Like little puppies they do not take their eyes from their master's hand to see if perhaps he may throw them a little morsel from his plate. So carefully do the poor follow my promptings that they listen to the wind (which blows where it pleases), even when it changes. From the sky they can read the weather and interpret the signs of the times. My grace is unpretentious, but the poor are satisfied with little gifts.

(*Fr Hans Urs von Balthasar*)

Here is also the perfect spot to pray the Third Mystery of Light - The Proclamation of the Kingdom of God.

⬝ FEEDING THE HUNGRY ⬝

"But they answered, 'All we have with us is five loaves and two fish'. So he said, 'Bring them here to me'." (*Mt* 14:17, 18)

"The miracle of the multiplication of loaves, when the Lord says the blessing, breaks and distributes the loaves through his disciples to feed the multitude, prefigures the superabundance of this unique bread of his Eucharist." (*CCC* 1335)

Tabgha

"When Jesus received this news [*of John the Baptist's beheading*] he withdrew by boat to a lonely place where they could be by themselves. But the crowds heard of this and, leaving the towns, went after him on foot. So as he stepped ashore he saw a large crowd;..." (*Mt* 14:13, 14). There is evidence, from tradition maintained by the early Judeo-Christian community, that Tabgha was 'the lonely place' on the shore of Lake Galilee to which Jesus withdrew.

This was reported by the pilgrim Egeria during her visit there in 383: "And in the same place by the sea is a grassy field with plenty of hay and many palm trees. By them are seven springs each flowing strongly. And this is the field where the Lord fed the people with five loaves and the two fishes. In fact the stone on which the Lord placed the bread has now been made into an altar. People who go there take away small pieces of the stone to bring them prosperity, and they are very effective. Past the walls of this church goes the public highway on which the Apostle Matthew had his place of custom."

Tabgha is an Arabic corruption of the Greek word *'heptapegon'* meaning seven springs, which although largely dry, are still identifiable today. Archaeologists have confirmed the presence of a primitive Syrian-style church building dating back to at least 350, of which remnants of its foundations can be seen under the glass cover next to the altar in the present church.

A larger Byzantine church was built over it around 450, which many pilgrims are reported to have visited, one being St Paula, guided by St Jerome, who called this place 'the solitude', in Greek *eremos*, the lonely place. This church was destroyed during the Persian invasion of 614, and lay in ruins for the next 1300 years as, unusually in the cycle of church regeneration in the Holy Land, there is no evidence of there having been a 12th century Crusader church on this site.

In 1886 the site was purchased by the German Catholic Association of the Holy Land, but it was not until 1932 that details of the previous churches emerged as the result of excavations by two German archaeologists. A temporary church was built in 1936 mainly to protect the ancient mosaics. The current church, the Church of the Multiplication, rebuilt on the same plan and in Byzantine style, was completed in 1982, and was consecrated by Cardinal Heffner of Cologne.

CHURCH OF THE MULTIPLICATION

In exterior, the church presents itself in the classical clean, clear-cut, bold and simple design lines of Byzantine - solid, reassuring, unfussy. Inside is similar. A simple, uncluttered three-naved church of pale stonework with a simple wood ceiling and beams. The naves are delineated by handsome, plain pillars with elaborately carved capitals, supporting wide arches. The bare stone apse only serves to emphasise the simple altar, under which lies the stone on which the loaves and fishes were reputed to have been placed.

In front of the altar is the famous 5th century loaves-and-fishes mosaic, iconic of the Holy Land and reproduced on a myriad commercial goods widely on sale. Intriguingly, only four loaves are shown in the mosaic, and whilst this miracle is clearly a pre-figuration of Jesus feeding His Church, it is said that

the fifth, missing loaf, specifically denotes the
Eucharist, which is with us until the end of time. The
other mosaics for which this church is so well known
are either side of the altar, depicting a free-field
Nilotic landscape, with associated flora and fauna, and
probably influenced by one of the patrons of the 5th
century church, Patriarch Martyrios of Jerusalem,
previously a monk of Egyptian training.

It is all set in very pleasant surroundings, which
include courtyard, cloister, shop and toilets. The
adjacent Benedictine monastery affords holidays for
disabled young people.

Miracle of the loaves and fishes

*"After this, Jesus crossed the Sea of Galilee - or
Tiberias - and a large crowd followed him,
impressed by the signs he had done in curing the
sick. Jesus climbed the hillside and sat down there
with his disciples. The time of the Jewish Passover
was near. Looking up, Jesus saw the crowds
approaching and said to Philip, 'Where can we buy
some bread for these people to eat?' He said this
only to put Philip to the test; he himself knew
exactly what he was going to do. Philip answered,
'Two hundred denarii would not buy enough to
give them a little piece each.' One of his disciples,
Andrew, Simon Peter's brother, said, 'Here is a*

Church of the Multiplication - 5th century loaves and fishes mosaic.

small boy with five barley loaves and two fish; but what is that among so many?' Jesus said to them, 'Make the people sit down.' There was plenty of grass there, and as many as five thousand men sat down. Then Jesus took the loaves, gave thanks, and distributed them to those who were sitting there; he did the same thing with the fish, distributing as much as they wanted. When they had eaten enough, he said to the disciples, 'Pick up the pieces left over, so that nothing is wasted.' So they picked them up and filled twelve large baskets with scraps left over from the meal of five barley loaves. Seeing the sign that he had done, the people said, 'This is indeed the prophet who is to come into the world.' Jesus, as he realised they were about to come and take him by force and make him king, fled back to the hills alone." (Jn 6:1-15)

Meditation

As for its being mentioned that Jesus lifted up his eyes and saw the multitude coming toward him, this is an indication of the divine benevolence, for he is wont to come by the grace of heavenly mercy to meet all those seeking to come to him. And lest they be able to go astray in their search, he is accustomed to open up the light of his Spirit to those hurrying to him.

As to Our Lord's asking Philip, in order to test him, 'Where shall we buy bread that these may eat?', this he doubtless did by his provident dispensation, not to learn something that he did not know, but so that Philip might recognise the sluggishness of his faith. His master knew of this, but he did not. Having been tested, he can recognise the truth, and, the miracle done he can amend. For he ought not to have doubted that with the presence of the Creator of all things, who brings forth bread from the earth and gladdens the hearts of human beings with wine, bread which could be bought for a few denarii was sufficient for a crowd of several thousands, so that all might receive what was sufficient and go away satisfied.

The five loaves of bread with which he satisfied the multitude of people are the five books of Moses. If they are opened up by spiritual understanding, and then multiplied by penetration of their deeper meaning, they daily refresh the hearts of the believers who hear them.

(*Bede the Venerable*)

≈ INVESTITURE OF PETER ≈

*"'Lord, you know everything; you know I love you.'
Jesus said to him, 'Feed my sheep'." (Jn 21:17)*

*"The sole Church of Christ [is that] which Our
Saviour, after His Resurrection, entrusted to
Peter's pastoral care, commissioning him and the
other apostles to extend and rule it..." (CCC 816)*

Peter's Primacy

Just a very short walking distance from the Church of
the Multiplication is the small Franciscan church of
Peter's Primacy, or *Mensa Christi*, the Table of
Christ. It is perched right on the lake's edge, set in
lovely, peaceful gardens. The history of churches on
this site is not precise. There is but scant evidence of
a 4th century building being here - possibly, part of it
being ancient steps cut in the lakeside rock as
reported by Egeria: "not far away from there [*altar of
Multiplication*] are some stone steps where the Lord
stood". In the 9th and 12th centuries there were
church buildings here which fell into ruins after the
defeat of the Crusaders. The Franciscans built the
present church in 1933, refurbishing in 1984. It is
built in the sombre black basalt rock of the region - in

Church of Peter's Primacy - with 'Egeria's steps'.

complete contrast to the many pale coloured churches in the Holy Land.

The setting of this church commemorates three particular events in the New Testament. Firstly, in a more general sense, it was just such a place as this that Jesus would have got into a boat and moved away from the water's edge so that he could effectively address the large crowds that gathered for His teachings: "Again he began to teach them by the lakeside, but such a huge crowd gathered round him that he got into a boat on the water and sat there. The whole crowd were at the lakeside on land" (*Mk* 4:1).

Here too the occasion is remembered when Jesus revealed Himself again to the Apostles after the Resurrection - when directing the Apostles' unsuccessful fishing to fruition, "Throw the net out to starboard and you'll find something" (*Jn* 21:6), and where He fed them with grilled fish and bread, "Come and have breakfast" (*Jn* 21:12). And lastly, part of this is the very beautiful and painful, but powerful, sequence where Peter thrice protests his love of the Lord in a heart-rending echo of his previous thrice denial, to which Jesus responds by commissioning him to lead His Church with the triple investiture, ending with "Feed my sheep".

MENSA CHRISTI

Inside, the church is very simple. Vivid, modern, stained glass windows, with the black, unadorned stone walls contrasting starkly with the plain whitewashed apse. Astride the sanctuary is the large natural rock feature where tradition has it that Jesus cooked the fish at that breakfast (*Mensa Christi*). A simple, rough pale stone-slabbed floor complements the whole: exquisite in its simplicity. Outside, close to the water's edge is a modern, dramatic statue of Jesus commissioning Peter: Jesus standing over Peter, hand outstretched; Peter kneeling and gazing up into Jesus' face; both holding a shepherd's crook in a symbolic hand-over from the Divine Shepherd to the first earthly one. Pope Paul VI made a point of visiting this church during his whirlwind tour of 1964.

Just opposite the main door, set under a large, shady tree, is a small amphitheatre round a stone altar where Mass can be celebrated. And in this quite stunning setting, one's gaze falls onto the altar on which lies the consecrated Eucharist, and then beyond, to the blue, glittering Sea of Galilee reflecting the Man and those events so many hundreds of years ago.

'Feed my sheep'

*"When they had eaten, Jesus said to Simon Peter,
'Simon, son of John, do you love me more than these
others do?' He answered, 'Yes, Lord, you know I
love you.' Jesus said to him, 'Feed my lambs.' A
second time he said to him, 'Simon son of John, do
you love me?' He replied, 'Yes, Lord, you know I
love you.' Jesus said to him, 'Look after my sheep.'
Then he said to him a third time, 'Simon son of
John, do you love me?' Peter was hurt that he had
asked him a third time, 'Do you love me?' and said,
'Lord, you know everything; you know I love you.'
Jesus said to him, 'Feed my sheep.'"* (Jn 21:15-17)

Meditation

For the Fathers of the Church, the parable of the
lost sheep, which the shepherd seeks in the desert,
was an image of the mystery of Christ and the
Church. The human race - every one of us - is the
sheep lost in the desert which no longer knows the
way. The Son of God will not let this happen; he
cannot abandon humanity in so wretched a
condition. He leaps to his feet and abandons the
glory of heaven, in order to go in search of the
sheep and pursue it, all the way to the Cross. He
takes it upon his shoulders and carries our

humanity; he carries us all - he is the good
shepherd who lays down his life for the sheep...

The symbol of the lamb also has a deeper
meaning. In the Ancient Near East, it was customary
for kings to style themselves shepherds of their
people. This was an image of their power, a cynical
image: to them their subjects were like sheep, which
the shepherd could dispose of as he wished.

When the shepherd of all humanity, the living
God, himself became a lamb, he stood on the side
of the lambs, with those who are downtrodden and
killed. This is how he reveals himself to be the true
shepherd: 'I am the Good Shepherd....I lay down
my life for the sheep,' Jesus says of himself (*Jn*
10:14). It is not power, but love that redeems us!
This is God's sign: He himself is love....God, who
became a lamb, tells us that the world is saved by
the Crucified One, not by those who crucified him.
The world is redeemed by the patience of God. It is
destroyed by the impatience of man.

One of the basic characteristics of a shepherd
must be to love the people entrusted to him, even
as he loves Christ whom he serves. 'Feed my
sheep,' says Christ to Peter: Feeding means loving,
and loving also means being ready to suffer.
Loving means giving the sheep what is truly good,

the nourishment of God's truth, of God's word, the nourishment of his presence, which he gives us in the Blessed Sacrament. (*Pope Benedict XVI*)

Jesus travelled widely in the course of His ministry and it was not all confined to the Galilee area. This included frequent visits to Jerusalem. In what has been described as His 'Sixth Journey', and about six months before His Passion and final journey to Jerusalem, He took three of His Disciples up Mount Tabor to witness His Transfiguration, which is described in the next Chapter. About eight days before the Transfiguration He made the first prophecy of the Passion: "The Son of Man is destined to suffer grievously, to be rejected by the elders and chief priests and scribes and to be put to death, and to be raised up on the third day." (*Lk* 9:22)

∼ TRANSFIGURATION ∼

"There in their presence he was transfigured: his face shone like the sun and his clothes became as dazzling as light". (Mt 17:2)

"On the threshold of the public life: the baptism; on the threshold of the Passover: the Transfiguration. Jesus' baptism proclaimed 'the mystery of the first regeneration', namely, our Baptism; the Transfiguration 'is the sacrament of the second regeneration': our own Resurrection. From now on we share in the Lord's resurrection through the Spirit who acts in the sacraments of the Body of Christ. The Transfiguration gives us a foretaste of Christ's glorious coming, when he 'will change our lowly body to be like his glorious body'. But it also recalls that 'it is through many persecutions that we must enter the kingdom of God.'" (CCC 556)

Mount Tabor

A few kilometres east of Nazareth, on the plain of Jezreel, stands Mount Tabor. This quite regular, domed mountain, is about 550 metres high, and dominates the flat, fertile plain around it. Although not mentioned specifically as the Transfiguration site -

referred to by Matthew only as 'a high mountain' - Tabor is the traditional place, being established by the 4th century, possibly through the influence of St Cyril of Jerusalem, who preferred it over one of the other possible sites, Mt Hermon, up to the north. Egeria certainly visited both: "Mount Tabor is much higher and loftier than Hermon, and from it can be seen the whole of Galilee and the Sea of Tiberias. These two mountains face each other".

But because of its strategic position over the surrounding area and being astride the ancient east/west trade routes, its recorded history goes back far. In 2000 BC the Caananites established a place of worship to their god Baal; *Psalm 89*, the hymn and prayer to God the faithful, acknowledges its significance and beauty, "you created the north and the south, Tabor and Hermon hail your name with joy" (v 12). *Judges 4* recalls the prophetess Deborah's call to arms in the mid 12th century BC to the general Barak: "Has not Yahweh, God of Israel, commanded, Go! March to Mount Tabor and with you take ten thousand of the sons of Naphtali and Zebulun" (v 6), where the Caananite chariots of Sisera were routed, and "not one man was spared" (v 16). Today's Arab village, Daburieh or Dabburiyah, at the western foot of the mountain, commemorates to this day, Deborah and Barak's victory here (see also *Judges 5*, the Song of Deborah and Barak). To the Arabs it was known as the *Jebel Tor* - mountain of the Bull.

Early churches

In the 3rd century BC a Seleucid fortress occupied the site; it was re-fortified by the Jewish commander Josephus for the First Jewish revolt in 66, which fell to the Roman commander, Vespasian, at which Josephus being so devastated by this defeat, joined the Roman army! The site then followed the expected pattern of occupation and reoccupation over the intervening centuries: in the 6th century there were, as recorded by the Anonymous Pilgrim of Piacenza, three churches on the summit; destruction by the Persians in 614; a fortress and monastery for the Benedictines built by Tancred the Crusader in 1099; the Byzantine church replaced by a Romanesque, three aisled basilica during the 12th century; successive occupation by the Saracens, Franks and Mamluks until the 17th century, when the Ottomans granted possession to the Franciscans in 1631; Napoleon defeated the Turks here in 1799. Work on the ruined Crusader church started in 1858, but it was not until 1924 that the present church, designed by Barluzzi to a Byzantine basilica style, was built over the 12th century building - a not insignificant achievement over all the ages, considering the effort required in hauling the building materials to the top!

There is a narrow hair-pinned road up to the summit, up which only cars or minibuses are permitted; coach tours have to debus and be taken up by the efficient and constant taxi shuttle. The site itself is level and quite extensive. Entrance is through a stone archway called the Gate of the Winds, and of which there are remnants of the defensive wall built by Josephus in the 1st century. Further along the driveway on the left can be seen the Greek Orthodox Church of Elijah, built in 1911; it is often closed to the public. Within the entrance gates of the Franciscan site, on the approaches to the main basilica, are the ruins of the 12th century Benedictine monastery, and on the left the outline of a small 6th century chapel, identifiable by its eastern apse.

BASILICA OF THE TRANSFIGURATION

The basilica is a handsome, pale-stoned church, standing square and solid at the far end of the plateau. The pillared and arched entrance is flanked by two sturdy, square towers. The front façade is an intriguing combination of the circular and square, the pillar and the portico, fronted by the enigmatic 'blind', small-apertured windows typical of a

Church of Transfiguration - crypt sanctuary.

Crusader church. Inside it is stunning, and a visual feast. The main impact is its simplicity, combined with its ingenious interior design: with the nave at a middle level, being able to look up to a galleried high altar, and below, in full view, the crypt chapel. It is light, cool, lofty and elegant. The apexed ceiling is criss-crossed with pale wooden beams, in turn supported by rows of delicate stone pillars. There are ample windows at this high level which let in the flood of light to this church.

The two side naves are separated with graceful square pillars and arches. The floor is a simple pattern in predominantly light-coloured marble. The radiant apse mosaic of the Transfiguration, over the main altar, literally glows. Jesus in the centre, Peter on the left, James and John on the right, and above them on clouds, Moses and Elijah. There are two side chapels on the same level as the main altar, that on the left dedicated to Our Lady, in which the Blessed Sacrament can be found, and that on the right, to St Francis. The long, barrel vaulted, mosaiced crypt sanctuary underneath is also very striking in its simplicity and its beauty, with its dazzling semi-circular stained glass window directly behind the altar, showing two peacocks - symbols of eternity - flanking a chalice. The two small side chapels under the two towers are dedicated to Moses and Elijah.

Just outside and to the right of the entrance is a viewing platform affording a magnificent panorama of the plain of Jezreel, showing clearly why it is called the 'bread basket of Israel', and emphasising why this feature held such strategic importance.

This is a site well worth visiting: in this high, lonely place is this beautiful church set in ancient and peaceful surroundings, which although at times can be busy, gives us every cue and assistance to meditating on the Transfiguration.

The Transfiguration

"Six days later, Jesus took with him Peter and James and his brother John and led them up a high mountain by themselves. There in their presence he was transfigured: his face shone like the sun and his clothes became as dazzling as light. And suddenly Moses and Elijah appeared to them; they were talking with him. Then Peter spoke to Jesus, 'Lord,' he said, 'it is wonderful for us to be here; if you want to, I will make three shelters here, one for you, one for Moses and one for Elijah.' He was still speaking when suddenly a bright cloud covered them with shadow, and suddenly from the cloud there came a voice which said, 'This is my Son, the Beloved; he enjoys my favour. Listen to him.' When they heard this the disciples fell on

their faces, overcome with fear. But Jesus came up and touched them, saying, 'Stand up, do not be afraid.' And when they raised their eyes they saw no one but Jesus." (*Mt* 17:1-8)

Meditation

Is it true that happiness cannot be found through purely human means? I loathe this way of posing the problem because we seem to be introducing God from the outside. Man cannot shift for himself, God comes to his rescue, puts his finger in the system. That is not at all what we see in the case of Father Maximilian Kolbe*. On the contrary, he makes us feel that God reveals himself through transfiguration. When Father Kolbe reaches the summit of the gift of himself, of this stupendous gift which makes him the champion of generosity, we feel he is profoundly human. Hence, to be fully human means to be transparent to God. When man is transfigured by this divine thought, he lets it show through himself, that is the moment one can truly speak of humanity. Therefore, we must not oppose God against human ways, because human ways are truly human only through this contact with God. And since, before this transfiguration, God is unknowable to us, we can

know God only through this transfiguration of man,
as man is truly man only at the moment he
surrenders himself to this dialogue of love by
losing himself in God. (*Fr Maurice Zundel*)

* St Maximilian Kolbe gave his life for another man in the
Auschwitz concentration camp.

Here also, is the perfect place to pray the Fourth
Mystery of Light - the Transfiguration.

On to Jerusalem

*"Now it happened that as the time drew near for
him to be taken up, he resolutely turned his face
towards Jerusalem..."* (*Lk 9:51*)

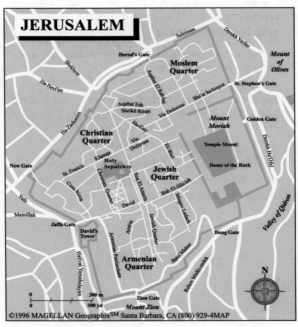

Jerusalem, Old City.

❦ MINISTRY ❦
IN JERUSALEM

❧ Jerusalem ❧

"Rather be joyful, be glad for ever
at what I am creating,
for look, I am creating Jerusalem to be 'Joy'
and my people to be 'Gladness'." (Is 65:18)

Turbulent history

Jerusalem has a rich, ancient and extremely turbulent history. Through its unique geographical, religious and political placement in this part of the world: for this is where the 'tectonic plates' of three major faiths, with their accompanying supporters of differing political and territorial ambitions have ground together, overlapped, and more than occasionally experienced major eruptions over three millennia. It gives witness to extraordinary events, of which little abatement seems likely, even in modern times. It is a very precise, focussed place in a very large world. Here, the chosen tribe of Israel had its most sacred Temple housing the Ark of the Covenant. Here, Jesus Christ was crucified and rose again. And it is here that members of all three Faiths believe that Abraham prepared to sacrifice his only son, Isaac, over which place now stands the Muslim shrine, the Dome of the Rock, with its distinctive and

Dome of the Rock and Wailing Wall.

prominent gold dome; this place also commemorates
from where Mohammed rose on the ladder of light,
being escorted by the angel Gabriel, to experience a
foretaste of Paradise.

By some reckonings the city has been besieged on
more than fifty occasions, conquered thirty six times,
and suffered ten total destructions. But it is a City that
has endured all this, and the Holy Places are still there,
still substantially intact, still being visited, after 2000
years. So even if the future does look bleak at times,
one has to take a long term view, and be confident that
despite the human folly that so often prevails, God will
continue to protect this unique City and its peoples: it
is both paradox and irony that this sentiment is aspired
to, and professed by, all of the three major Faiths-in-
residence, with equal desire and intent.

There are traces of settlement in this area going
back to the Early Bronze Age (3-5000BC). Evidence
of a circa 2000 BC cemetery on the Mount of Olives
has been discovered, and whilst official
commemoration of the third millennium was
celebrated in Jerusalem in 1996, the first mention of it
in the Bible is from Abraham's time, circa 2000 BC,
when, "Melchizedek, king of Salem brought bread
and wine " (*Gn* 14:18). In *Ps* 76:2 we read, "God is
acknowledged in Judah, / his name is great in Israel, /
his tent is pitched in Salem, / his dwelling is in Zion".

Salem is recognised as the abridged name of Jerusalem, the city of peace, from the Hebrew *shalom*.

The Old City Today

Today's wider Jerusalem bears little resemblance to the Jerusalem of even 150 years ago, when there was very little development outside the City walls. It is only after the six-day war of 1967 that there has been development on a large scale, with Israeli government infrastructure and accompanying commercial and residential areas being built around the Old City. However, the Old City thankfully bears little sign of extensive modern development, and retains that vibrant, hectic, crowded, jostling, aromatic, heady atmosphere of a busy Middle East market town. It is an energising, fascinating place, with its narrow, polished, enclosed cobbled alleys, teeming with small shops and market stalls and all sorts of small businesses, all spilling out onto the walkways, creating a paradoxically intimate atmosphere.

Since the Old City is built on sloping ground, the alleys are mainly stepped and uneven - it is not easy to get about for those with limited agility. There could not be more of a contrast and mix of peoples anywhere else in the world. If you want to be totally absorbed in people-watching on a grand and noisy scale, go down from the Damascus Gate to the vicinity of El Wad

Street and the junction of the *Via Dolorosa*, where the
activity, cacophony and movement is on an operatic
and grand sensory level! There are quiet corners
however, where one can wander and absorb some
peaceful atmosphere, particularly in the Christian
Quarter around St Francis Street.

Getting to grips with the Old City is not difficult,
with its four distinct Quarters - Christian, Armenian,
Jewish, and Muslim. It is very compact, barely a square
kilometre in area, the streets mainly running east-west,
north south, although orientation can at times be tricky
in the crowded enclosed alleys when on the move! All
the pilgrim venues are either within the Old City, or
walkable on the outskirts. There are very acceptable
Christian hostels in the Old City, details of which can
be obtained from the Christian Information Centre by
the Jaffa Gate; there is also a general Tourist
Information Centre by the Jaffa Gate. At some stage of
your stay, it would be well worth walking the ramparts
of the Old City, which can be accessed from the Jaffa
or Damascus gates. It not only offers a good view and
perspectives onto the Old City, along with some rather
eccentric roofing arrangements, but also extensive
aspects of the wider Jerusalem and surrounding vistas.

There are several separate areas in which places of
interest can conveniently be grouped together and
explored and experienced, and they are described in

the following chapters: The Church of the Holy Sepulchre, The Mount of Olives on the eastern side, the Mount Zion area immediately to the south of the Zion Gate, various bits and pieces in and around that can be taken up as your programme allows, and the *Via Dolorosa* (Stations of the Cross) running through the Old City.

Jerusalem

*Jerusalem, take off your dress
of sorrow and distress,
Put on the beauty of God's glory
for evermore,
Wrap the cloak of God's saving justice
around you,
Put the diadem of the Eternal One's
glory on your head,
For God means to show your splendour
to every nation under heaven,
And the name God
gives you for evermore will be,
'Peace-through-Justice
and Glory-through-Devotion'.
(Ba 5:1-4)*

❦ THE CHURCH ❦
OF THE HOLY SEPULCHRE

Golgotha

This quite extraordinary church complex marks the place where Jesus was crucified and laid to rest in the tomb. For those many of us who are conditioned by the many depictions of the Crucifixion scene being set on a prominent but barren and stark hilltop, be prepared to adjust to what you will see when you enter the Church of the Holy Sepulchre. And because of what this place is - the most important site in Christendom - it has suffered the extravagances of human attention throughout its existence, from savage desecration, lavish restoration, piecemeal preservation, to over-zealous protection and over-adornment. Where I have described Jerusalem as the 'tectonic plates' of the three great monotheistic faiths, the Holy Sepulchre is where the many 'sub plates' of the early Churches of Christendom grind together and occasionally erupt.

But within this contemporary cityscape there is strong traditional, historical and archaeological evidence that supports this area as being the site of Crucifixion and burial of Christ. Firstly, the oral evidence about this place would have been faithfully preserved and widely made known by the followers of

Jesus who witnessed His burial and Resurrection - Mary Magdalene, Mary the mother of James, 'took note of the tomb, and how he had been laid' (*Lk* 23:55); Peter and John 'saw the linen cloths lying on the ground' (*Jn* 20:5); not to mention the Roman soldiers, seeing the empty tomb, 'went off into the city to tell the chief priests all that had happened' (*Mt* 28:11).

The tomb, belonging to Joseph of Aramathea, would also no doubt have been kept in his family's hands, and would have remained as a place of veneration to believers, or one of just curiosity to non-believers. It is also important to bear in mind that Jesus' followers expected the Second Coming within their lifetime, hence places such as this were not then formally marked for future generations, as indeed Jesus' teachings were not formally committed to writing in the New Testament, until succeeding generations realised the need to record and mark these events and places in order to pre-empt any dilution or loss of the oral tradition.

History

Destruction

In 70 AD the Emperor Titus destroyed Jerusalem and the Jewish Temple in response to the first Jewish uprising, and it lay in ruins for decades after that, a potent fulfilment of Jesus' prophecy 'that not one stone would be left upon another' (*Lk* 19:44). The Crucifixion site, however, being a burial ground and away from human habitation at that time, may not have been directly affected; similarly the fledgling Christian community under James the Less as its first bishop, with its memories of these places, survived.

Any subsequent re-population of Jerusalem was again forestalled by the Emperor Hadrian in repressing the second Jewish Revolt in 135. He rebuilt Jerusalem in the typical style of a Roman colonial town, naming it *Aelia Capitolina*. Over the rough, uneven ground of the hillock of Calvary, and the tomb close by in the hillside, he built an extensive level podium on which were placed a statue of Jupiter and a temple to Venus. As St Jerome observed in the 4th century this 'cover up' had the opposite effect of continuing to indicate exactly where these holy sites were.

Constantine's church

Constantine, the first Christian Roman Emperor, ordered the search for Calvary, expressing his wish to 'make that most blessed spot, the place of the Resurrection, visible to all and given over to veneration'. In 325 this work commenced, exposing

Calvary again and the tomb. In order to fulfil Constantine's express instructions that the site be adorned 'with splendid buildings', the whole site had to be levelled but still ingeniously retaining the height of Calvary, whilst allowing the burial tomb to remain in its original rock setting, the surrounding hill having been removed and levelled. Eusebius, the Bishop of Caesarea who observed all this, wrote, 'Is it not astonishing to see the rock standing isolated, in the midst of a level space, with a cave inside it?'.

Constantine's 4th century church was much the largest building to stand on this site, and consisted principally of a large Rotunda around the tomb, which itself was adorned with an ornate edicule, and designated the Anastasis or Church of the Resurrection, with close by, the Basilica of Constantine, or Martyrium - Place of Witness - marking the site of Calvary. Between and around the two main buildings were courts, colonnaded areas and other subsidiary buildings. The Basilica was consecrated in 335 in the presence of 300 Bishops, fulfilling Constantine's desire for a powerful and enduring focus for Christian pilgrimage.

Troubled times

The 7th century saw troubled times over the whole land with invasion and destruction by the Persians

in 614, including Constantine's church. Only a few
years afterwards, the Persians were driven out by
the Roman Emperor Heraclius, who ordered the site
to be rebuilt under the direction of Bishop
Modestus. In 637 the City was overrun by the
Muslims, but the church was spared by their leader
Caliph Omar, allowing Christians to continue
worshipping there. Sadly, in 1009 the Holy
Sepulchre became the focus for destruction of
Christian churches by the fanatical Caliph Hakim,
and the Basilica and Martyrium were levelled to the
ground, and lay in ruins for almost forty years. In a
deal involving Muslim prisoners, Monomachus, the
Roman Emperor started rebuilding on the site in
1048, but on a reduced and modest scale.

It was not until the Crusaders who captured the
City in 1099 that total and ambitious restoration of
the church commenced, employing the finest
craftsmen from all over Europe. Work on the church,
showing very much the same basic form that we see
today, was completed around 1180, although in July
1149 a joyful service of thanksgiving was held
celebrating the return of this holy place. The building
was spared by Saladin, the Muslim conqueror, in
1187; Eastern Christians were allowed to remain in
Jerusalem, the Latins were expelled, returning in
token in 1192, although Saladin resisted pressure

from the Orthodox to grant them sole ownership. The keys were given to Muslim custodians to hold, of which they still do today, having been passed on down two families through the many generations, with the Judah family holding the key, and the Nusseibehs turning it.

Over the next centuries the struggle for ownership and part-ownership swayed back and forth, depending who had favour with the ruling regime, be it in geo-political terms, or more practically, non-payment of taxes! Greeks, Latins, Georgians, Armenians, Jacobites, Copts and Ethiopians all had their stake in varying and fluctuating degrees. More detail over these machinations are given in the Introductory Chapter when discussing the 'Status Quo'. In 1808 a fire seriously damaged the Rotunda. Numerous problems and intrigues arose over the restoration. East-West relations were at a low ebb through the Napoleonic Wars, Palestine being ruled by the Turks. The major restoration was left to the Eastern Churches, who, frankly, did a poor job: many windows were filled in, the simple Crusader edicule was replaced with the current one, the tombs of the Crusader Kings of Jerusalem, and many other rich stone decorations, were removed. The church took on its present rather gloomy, fragmented appearance.

Thankfully, the more serious issues have receded, and whilst tensions and sensitivities regarding self-protection still prevail, there is a more ecumenical approach between the three major stakeholders: the Latins, the Greeks and the Armenians. Restoration and repair has proceeded, albeit at a snail's pace. In 1959 a common plan was agreed, and the redecoration of the Rotunda was finally completed in 1997 in time for Jerusalem's Jubilee celebrations.

CHURCH OF THE HOLY SEPULCHRE

The first glimpse of the main entrance façade is on entering the small forecourt, or parvis, from the narrow alleys of the surrounding *souk*. Like many Crusader churches it is built for strength rather than elegance, as is typified by the massive and ungainly, fortress-like bell tower to the left of the entrance; but to give its lack of proportion some due, the tower's height had to be reduced after an earthquake in the sixteenth century. There are side chapels on both sides of the parvis, but the instinct of the pilgrim will be to head straight into the Basilica, so we will come back to these later!

However, before entering, you will note that the right hand entrance is not in use, it having been blocked over in 1187, and you will also see some external stone steps to the right of the entrance, leading

Holy Sepulchre - exterior, parvis and main entrance.

up into a now closed porch area, which originally gave access to the Calvary chapel above. This porch beneath the small cupola is known as the Chapel of the Franks, and underneath that, at ground level, is a small Greek oratory dedicated to Mary of Egypt (to which there is no access either). Just in front of the central columned jamb to the main entrance, beneath wooden boards, is the tomb of Philip d'Aubigny, an English Crusader, Governor of the Channel Islands and tutor to Henry III, who died in 1236.

Inside the Bascilica

As you enter the Basilica, you may be excused some disorientation, partly from coming out of the brightness into this great gloomy cavern, but also because this is no conventional church - there is no recognisable layout or obvious focal point. Unless you are very early, there are also likely to be a crowd of people and a general hubbub. But before you go anywhere at all, just pause and take an overview of what you see immediately around you. The object of your attention immediately in front of you as you enter, is a polished, red limestone slab, mounted low at ground level, surrounded by tall candlesticks, over which eight devotional lamps hang.

Then, casting your eyes past this and upwards you will see a wall of mosaics, above which and beyond, there is a high rotunda. Over to your left, and still high up, is another, larger rotunda, supported by thick pillars, which from your current viewpoint partially obscure what is below, at floor level. Turning to your immediate right there is an ambulatory leading off, then a small under-chapel, and further round to your right rear, almost by the main entrance, an arched entrance through which some deep, steep steps climb, spiralling up.

There seems to be a dearth of clear, coherent stand-alone guide books to the Basilica - only brief descriptions with numbered floor plans. So a simple tour will have to suffice. You do need time to attune to this place. Take your time, take stock and reflect. Try and look beyond all the people and your pre-conceptions. So, before you move away from the entrance area, look immediately on the left and just inside the entrance. Here you will see the doorkeeper's bench, usually occupied by a representative from one of the same two Muslim families who have had custody of the doors, and are responsible for locking and unlocking it, since the Crusaders were defeated in 1187. If it is quiet, and you judge the moment right, you might engage in conversation. Ask to see the key, a large, rather unwieldy, un-keylike iron hook!

CRUCIFIXION

Calvary

Now climb the steep, wide spiral staircase immediately to the right of the main entrance. This takes you up to the Calvary hill top. As you emerge at this level, you will see to your right, two ornate, pillared-and-arched 'open-plan' chapels, side by side. The right hand chapel is Roman Catholic and presents the Eleventh Station of the Cross - Jesus is nailed to the Cross. The mosaic depicting this scene above the altar shows Jesus, prostrate on the grounded Cross. Mary Magdalene is weeping at His feet. The whole scene is overlooked by the gaunt and severe figure of Our Lady, her body rigid with pain and anticipation of what is to come. The vaulted ceiling and arches are richly decorated by mosaics. In the ceiling near the altar, darker than its surround, a figure of Jesus, being the only surviving Crusader mosaic in the building. Through the grille on the right can be seen the Chapel of the Franks, the original entrance to Calvary.

The Chapel to the left, the Calvary Chapel, is Greek Orthodox. It represents the place where Jesus was crucified; the Twelfth Station of the Cross. It presents a glorious and absolute glittering blaze of embossed silver panels behind the altar, beautiful silver life-sized icons of Our Lady, Saint John and

Holy Sepulchre - Golgotha.

Mary Magdalene, a myriad of gleaming silver and gold hanging lamps and chandeliers, burning candles, all dominated by a life-sized, iconic Christ hanging on the Cross. It is here that the pilgrim can kneel under the small altar at the foot of the Cross and touch, through the small circular hole at ground level, a piece of rock on which stood the Cross. The original rock face of Calvary can be seen through the glass panels on each side of the altar, as can the fissure caused by the earthquake when Jesus died.

Death

"When the sixth hour came there was darkness over the whole land until the ninth hour. And at the ninth hour Jesus cried out in a loud voice, 'Eloi, eloi, lama sabacthani?' which means, 'My God, my God, why have you forsaken me?' When some of those who stood by heard this, they said, 'Listen, he is calling on Elijah.' Someone ran and soaked a sponge in vinegar and, putting it on a reed, gave it to him to drink, saying, 'Wait! And see if Elijah will come to take him down.' but Jesus gave a loud cry and breathed his last. And the veil of the Sanctuary was torn in two from top to bottom. The centurion, who was standing in front of him, had seen how he had died and said, 'In truth, this man was Son of God.' (Mk 15:33-39)

Lament

"I am the man familiar with misery / under the rod of his fury. / He has led and guided me / into darkness, not light. / Against none but me does he turn his hand, / again and again, all day. / He has wasted my flesh and skin away, / has broken my bones. / He has besieged me and made hardship / a circlet round my head. / He has forced me to dwell where all is dark, / like those long-dead in their everlasting home. / He has walled me in so that I can not escape; / he has weighed me down with chains; / even when I shout for help, / he shuts out my prayer." (*Lm* 3:1-9)

Meditation

Jesus dies on the Cross. The culmination of evil and the eternal victory of Goodness coincide! He died for us that we might live! Every true good, every true love, every true life springs from this most blasphemous and most sacred moment. He has reconciled everything! Cloud and darkness are his raiment; his throne justice and right (cf *Ps* 97:2). There is no contradiction in God. He is Peace. (*Fr Richard Veras*)

3 O'clock Prayer

You expired, Jesus, but the source of life gushed forth for souls and the Ocean of Mercy opened up for the whole world. O Fount of Life, unfathomable Divine Mercy, envelope the whole world and empty yourself out upon us.

O Blood and Water which gushed forth from the Heart of Jesus as a Fount of Mercy for us, I trust in You. Jesus, I trust in You! (*Divine Mercy*)

Stabat Mater

In between these two chapels, at the front, is a small (Roman Catholic) altar to Our Lady of Sorrows, on which stands a rather lovely wooden, painted bust of the Sorrowful Mother, her heart being pierced with a sword, in Simeon's words to her, 'and a sword will pierce your soul too' (*Lk* 2:35). The statue was a gift from Queen Maria I of Portugal, presented in 1778.

Meditation

Mary is not just a Mother who is sorrowful because her Son is suffering. Standing at the foot of the Cross, Our Blessed Lady does not passively or even just patiently assist at the sacrifice of her Son.

In obedience to the Father's saving will, she gives up his and her Son. She gives, she offers; she does not merely let go. With love she says Yes to the immolation of the Victim who is flesh of her flesh, the fruit of her womb. (*John Saward*)

Here, pray also the Fifth Sorrowful Mystery of the Rosary - the Crucifixion and Death of Jesus.

Moving to the back of these two chapels, you can gaze over the balustrade at the church area below, to which you are about to descend and move through, going down the steep, straight staircase, at the back-left of the chapels.

Chapel of Adam and Stone of Anointing

Now that you have descended back to ground level, turn immediately into the small chapel directly underneath Calvary. This is the Chapel of Adam, where Greek Orthodox tradition has it that Adam was buried in a cave below Golgotha, and his remains were the first over which the redemptive blood of Jesus flowed from the Cross above. Hence the Greek Orthodox depiction of the Crucifix often shows a skull at Jesus' feet. By the entrance of the Chapel were once the tombs of the first Crusader kings, Godfrey of Bouillon and Baldwin I, they having been plundered during the Turkish invasion of 1244. Just outside this chapel, one can again view behind glass and at a lower level, the original rock and earthquake fissure of the Crucifixion site.

From Adam's Chapel you can now turn your attention to the low, limestone slab that caught your eye on entering the Sepulchre. It denotes and symbolises the place where Jesus' body, having been taken down from the Cross, was laid and anointed for burial. It is known as the Stone of Anointing or Unction. The Thirteenth Station, Jesus is taken down from the Cross, is remembered here. The current slab replaced a twelfth century slab which was destroyed in 1808. On the wall above and behind are some splendid modern, iconic mosaics showing the sequence of Jesus being taken down from the Cross, anointed, and laid in the Tomb.

RESURRECTION

Rotunda: the Tomb

In moving on to your left, to the area of the huge, pillared, star-emblazoned Rotunda, we now need to take the next overview. The focal point, in the centre, is Jesus' Tomb. With this blunt realisation, and having to take in what you are looking at, will no doubt stir many emotions. For what you actually see is a large grimy, inelegant edifice, blighted by ugly steel girders on the outside, on which haphazardly burn many devotional candles. What with the smoke, general gloom and hubbub of the whole place, it can sometimes give an impression of something reminiscent from the Industrial Revolution! However, early in the morning, or late at night, it can be profoundly peaceful. Nonetheless, this is the holiest site of Christendom where Jesus was laid to rest amongst great distress and mourning, and from where, three days later, He rose in glory to give Light to the world.

As we work our way round the Tomb, we will continue to maintain our view of the wider scene: over to your left (and rear) you will see quite a small, free standing structure of four slim, elegant pillars supporting a circular marble canopy. This area is known as the Place of Mourning, from which 'many women were there, watching from a distance' (*Mt* 27:55) and looking on in sorrow. This area is owned by the Armenians, as evidenced by their sacristy behind, and some stairs leading up to their living quarters and private oratory. The massive Rotunda itself, or *Anastasis* (Resurrection), is built on the foundations of the Constantinian church, the western half of which faithfully duplicates the original shape and form. Originally the pillars were covered in marble, and the cupola gleamed and shone with rich mosaics. The current dome was completed by 1980, and the twelve pointed star, whose rays symbolise the outreach of the twelve apostles, was finished in 1997.

Coptic and Jacobite chapels

Before concentrating on the Tomb itself, continue to wander slowly, clockwise, round the Tomb area, if only to start to get your head round it all and absorb the whole. At the rear, looking as though it has been 'tacked on' to the back of the Tomb, is what can only be described as a nomad's chapel, with a really rather ad hoc look about it. But it is charming, and has a bright air about it. It is the Chapel owned and manned by the monks of the Coptic Church. To me it conjures up lovely images of these nomadic people taking their most holy chapel with them, and setting it up with joy and reverence, whenever they have the opportunity. However, this small Chapel has been in situ, with its faithful monks, since the sixteenth century!

Coptic Incense Prayer

O King of Peace, give us your peace and pardon our sins. Dismiss the enemies of the Church and protect her so that she may never fail. Emmanuel our God is in our midst in the glory of the Father and of the Holy Spirit. May he bless us and purify our hearts and cure the sicknesses of our soul and body. We adore you, O Christ, with your good Father and the Holy Spirit because you have come and you have saved us.

At the very back of the Rotunda, directly opposite the Coptic Chapel, you can pass through two of the supporting pillars into a small, rudimentary dilapidated chapel. Ownership is claimed by the Armenians, but is used by the Syrian-Jacobites; it is dedicated to Ss Joseph of Arimathea & Nicodemus. It is not in regular use, but the small ramshackle altar remains in place to maintain claim of ownership. The curved wall at the back of the Chapel is part of one of the three-apsed chapels of the original Constantinian church. However, what leads off from this chapel is of extreme archaeological importance in supporting the claim that this area was a burial site outside the city walls at the time of Jesus. This small complex, hewn out of the original bedrock, presents two first century Jewish tombs - which under Jewish law for burial, would not have been placed within the city walls, or any built-up area. It is amazing that a place of such consequence is presented and maintained in such a low-key, offhand fashion, as the tombs are likely to be those of the family of Joseph of Arimathea.

Catholicon

It is now time to complete your circuit of the Tomb, and prepare to enter it. In busy periods there will be a system of queuing and queue control; this may seem over officious, and there may be a period of waiting. As you wait, take in the splendid *Catholicon*, by the front of the Tomb. Although access into this area appears restricted, one can enter with permission from the Greek Orthodox priests on duty. This area, the choir of the Crusader church, has now been adapted, with the original transepts having been walled-in on both sides. It now takes the Greek Orthodox style, with the ornately decorated and icon clad *iconostasis* partially obscuring the high altar. High above is the cupola you first saw when you entered the Basilica, from which hangs an impressive chandelier. Under the cupola, on the floor, is a marble circle, an *'omphalos'* meaning 'navel'. At the time of Jesus, Jerusalem was called 'the Belly of the Universe' where the tombs of the First and Second Adam were to be found; the place of human redemption and resurrection - the place where the Father's son was sacrificed, not Abraham's, but God's.

The Tomb of the Resurrection

Turning back now to the Tomb. The present structure, or edicule, described as a Muscovite cupola, is built in marble and was erected in 1810 by the Greek and

Holy Sepulchre - the Tomb of the Resurrection.

Russian Orthodox. The steel girders were inserted by British Royal Engineers to shore it up after an earthquake in 1927. It certainly lies on the site of the first-century cave tomb, preserved by Constantine. It is of course, the final Station of the Cross. The entrance is flanked by massive candlesticks and overhung with an elaborate array of devotional lamps. A large painting of the Risen Christ, is mounted high above, on the top balustrade.

The tomb itself is divided into the traditional two chambers, the first serving as a porch and meeting place for mourners, the second where the body was laid. The first chamber, designated the Chapel of the Angel, commemorates where the angel announced the Resurrection, 'There is no need to be amazed. You are looking for Jesus of Nazareth, who was crucified: he has risen, he is not here. See, here is the place where they laid him.' (*Mk* 16:6); it is ornate, elegantly pillared, bedecked with lamps, and marble lined. In the centre is a small altar, or pilaster, said to be formed from part of the large stone that was rolled away from the entrance to the Tomb. There is an ornately carved and low entrance into the burial chamber.

Inside it is small - room for three, and because of time and space constraints, it was difficult at the time to make anything hugely meaningful of it all, other than briefly kneel at the raised marble bench and slab where Jesus was laid, and just embrace it, with huge, probably undefined, emotion. My memory of this first visit is hazy, but the impression of the cramped, brightly be-candled and lavishly decorated space will be in my mind for ever. If you are staying in Jerusalem take the opportunity to come back to the Resurrection tomb before breakfast or after dinner, when it is quiet.

Franciscan Chapel of the Apparition

Having been into the tomb, my next impulse now was to move across to the far side of the Rotunda into the Franciscan Chapel, dedicated to the Apparition of Jesus to His Mother. This Chapel commemorates the tradition that Jesus appeared to Mary separately after the Resurrection. If not being used for a service, it is a lovely quiet corner in which to escape and pray, and to settle your mind and spirit after the very mixed emotions of your recent visit to Calvary and the Tomb, the more so, as Jesus is here, present in the Blessed Sacrament. It is a twelfth century Chapel, largely unchanged since Crusader days, and lovingly and tastefully maintained by the Franciscans.

It is very plain, bare-stoned, with a high, barrelled roof. You see a dramatic bas relief of Jesus appearing to Our Lady, a plain blue and glinting gold-chipped mosaic apse, and a powerful globe-shaped tabernacle, surrounded by the Cross. On the left, up on a ledge, in a continuous procession of small, bronze statuettes, is a striking presentation of the Stations of the Cross. By the door, there is a fragment of a pillar said to be the one at which Jesus was scourged, which was revered on Mount Zion in the fourth century, and brought here in the fourteenth.

Resurrection

"It was very early on the first day of the week and still dark, when Mary of Magdala came to the tomb. She saw that the stone had been moved away from the tomb and came running to Simon Peter and the other disciple, the one whom Jesus loved. 'They have taken the Lord out of the tomb,' she said, 'and we don't know where they have put him.' So Peter set out with the other disciple to go to the tomb. They ran together, but the other disciple, running faster than Peter, reached the tomb first; he bent down and saw the linen cloths lying on the ground, but did not go in. Simon Peter, following him, also came up, went into the tomb, saw the linen cloths lying on the ground and also the cloth that had been over his head; this was not with the linen cloths but rolled up in a place by itself. Then the other disciple who had reached the tomb first also went in; he saw and he believed. Till this

moment they had still not understood the scripture,
that he must rise from the dead." (Jn 20:1-9)

Meditation

Only a while ago you still knelt at the empty grave,
a sea of tears. And all you knew was that the Lord
was dead, that the life of quiet joy you shared was
dead. You only stare into the void of the cave. A
cold and chilly wind is exhaled from your soul,
where the dead man laid himself to rest, where you
embalmed and shrouded him with an awe that no
longer expects anything. You want to be in
attendance at his grave. You don't cease praying or
going to empty ceremonies in churches, to perform
a hopeless service for your dead love. And oh, what
is now the meaning of resurrection? Who can know
it from among those who have not themselves risen
from the dead? What is now the meaning of faith? It
has been sealed within the grave. What is now the
meaning of hope? A leaden thought with neither
power nor learning. And love? Alas, perhaps it is
now no more than sorrow, the empty pain of
disconsolate futility, the weariness that can no
longer mourn. And so you stare into the void. For in
fact: the grave is empty, you are yourself empty,
and are therefore, already pure, and only this staring

spasm keeps you from looking behind you. You stare ahead of you, and behind your back stands your Life! It calls to you, you turn around and cannot recognise it. Your eyes, unused to light can grasp nothing. And then an abrupt word: your name! Your own dear name coming from the mouth of Love: your being, your very essence - yourself! - bounding from the mouth thought dead...O word, O name, you, my own name! Spoken to me, breathed forth with a smile and a promise. O stream of light, O faith, hope, love! In a thunderclap I am the new creature (this I am, can be, am allowed to be). I am given back to myself, and then, at the very instant when I shout for joy, I cast myself down at the feet of Life. (*Fr Hans Urs von Balthasar*)

Prayer

"Open to me the gates of holiness: I will enter and give thanks. This is the Lord's own gate where the just may enter. I will thank you for you have answered and you are my saviour.

O Lord, grant us salvation; O Lord, grant success. Blessed in the name of the Lord is he who comes. We bless you from the house of the Lord; the Lord God is our light."
(*Ps* 118:19-21, 25-27)

Here, pray the First Glorious Mystery of the Rosary - the Resurrection.

OTHER CHAPELS

Leaving this Chapel you will see the Franciscan sacristy immediately on the left, and then to your front left against a pillar, the altar, and modern, bronze bas-relief of Jesus appearing to Mary Magdalene after the Resurrection (*'Noli me tangere*..do not cling to me'....*Jn* 20:17). Turning left here down the wide but rather gloomy ambulatory you will walk past some high arches, known as the Arches of the Virgin, which are made up of remains from earlier Basilicas. The wall to your right blocks off and encloses the Greek *Catholicon*, from what was once the open transepts to the 12th century Crusader church. The toilets are on the left at the start of the ambulatory - and should only be used in emergency - they are an absolute disgrace!

Side Chapels

Down at the end of this ambulatory, front left, is a small, Greek Chapel called the 'Prison of Christ'. There is a twelfth century tradition that Jesus and the two thieves were imprisoned here before the

Crucifixion, but is more likely to have developed as a liturgical station in commemorating the Passion. To the right of the Chapel, in a glass case, an ancient stone 'stocks' is on display - origin unknown.

Moving on round this ambulatory you will then come to the next side chapel on your left, belonging to the Greeks, and dedicated to St Longinus, the Roman soldier who 'pierced his side with a lance; and immediately there came out blood and water' (*Jn* 19:34). Tradition recounts that he was blind in one eye, but was cured by the water and blood flowing from Christ's side, and through this miracle was converted. The Chapel next to this is the Armenian Chapel of the Division of the Robes.

Move now down the 29 steps of the wide stairway just to the left of this Chapel, to the splendid, spacious Armenian Chapel of St Helena. As you go down, notice on the left hand wall the many crosses that were carved by medieval pilgrims.

St Helena

Whilst there is some evidence from the north and south foundations that this was the crypt of the Constantinian Basilica, it is more likely to have been built by the Crusaders in the early 12th century. This three aisled church, with its two apses, elegant columns and arches, is richly decorated, and displays many large dramatic pictures and murals from Armenian Church history and tradition. The altar on the left is dedicated to St Dismas, the Penitent Thief. As his life ebbed away in agony, he pleaded in humility and faith, 'Jesus, remember me when you come into your kingdom' (*Lk* 23:40-43). The right hand altar is dedicated to the Empress Helena. Note the dome above, letting natural light into the chapel, which you will come across again, outside, at 'ground' level.

Further stairs, in the right hand corner of this Chapel lead down to the Catholic Chapel of the Finding of the True Cross. Tradition has it that St Helena discovered the True Cross and the Instruments of the Passion, now displayed and venerated at the Basilica of the Holy Cross in Jerusalem in Rome (cf CTS booklet, *Rome, A Pilgrim's Companion*). Above the Catholic altar on the left is a statue of this event; the altar on the right is Greek.

Returning up the two flights of stairs, and turning left down the ambulatory, brings you to the third side Chapel in this part of the Basilica. This is the Greek Chapel of the Derision, or the Mocking of Our Lord. Continuing along the ambulatory soon brings you back to the protruding glass case displaying the Calvary rock by the Chapel of Adam, and back to the entrance.

Peripheries

Exploring the peripheries of the Church will prove just as fascinating, but not as time-consuming. Not all these places may necessarily be open, and you may have to seek entry. On the left hand side as you face the church (west) of the forecourt there are three Greek Orthodox chapels. The first is dedicated to St James the Less, first Bishop of Jerusalem. This is the Greek Orthodox Parish church; in the middle is the chapel of St John the Baptist, with its ancient baptistry; and at the end, under the belfry, is the chapel commemorating the Forty Martyrs, soldiers of the Roman Twelfth Legion serving in Armenia in 320 who were Christians. They were sentenced to being frozen to death by having to stand naked, in winter, on a frozen pond, rather than carry out the sacrifices to the Emperor as required by the Governor of the Province.

On the other side of the forecourt, the door furthest from the Basilica leads into the Greek Orthodox Convent of St Abraham (no access); the central arched doorway leads into the ornately decorated Armenian Chapel of St John; and the last, small door leads into the Chapel of St Michael, owned by the Copts, but used by the Ethiopian monks - from this chapel you can go upstairs to their upper chapel.

Of the all the exterior chapels I found these two the most charming, the most beguiling and the most intriguing. To me, the rather garish, over-the-top, but unpretentious presentation, was utterly authentic and seemed totally in context with the dignified Ethiopian monks and nuns who populate and pray in these places. If you are fortunate enough to be present when they are praying in community, leaning gracefully on their tall 'T' shaped sticks, and chanting their prayer, you will get that tingling feeling of being with faithful followers of Christ untouched by time or modern temperament.

Leaving their upper chapel at this level will again give you quite a surprise. For, not only do you find yourself on the 'roof' of the large, domed Armenian Chapel to St Helena, but you will also be forgiven for thinking you have somehow arrived in a small slice of Africa, because it is on this rooftop courtyard that the Ethiopian monks and nuns live in their very distinctive and simple monastery buildings. There will invariably be one of their monks present in that area, and again if you judge it to be right, engage in conversation, and ask for a blessing as you part company. If you follow the *Via Dolorosa*, after the ninth Station you will enter this courtyard from the alley way in the opposite direction, and again quite unexpectedly come across this charming scene (see separate Chapter on *Via Dolorosa*).

Syro-Maronite Farewell to the Altar

Remain in peace, O Altar of God. May the offering I have taken from you be for the remission of my debts and the pardon of my sins, and may it obtain for me that I may stand before the tribunal of Christ without condemnation and without confusion. I do not know if I will have the opportunity to return and offer another sacrifice upon you. Protect me, O Lord, and preserve your holy Church as the way to truth and salvation. Amen.

✄ MOUNT OF OLIVES ✄

The Mount of Olives is the high feature to the east of Old Jerusalem, separated from the City by the Kidron Valley below, and from it, allowing some wonderful panoramic views of the Old City. It is rich in New Testament activity, but it is mentioned well before then in the Old Testament, in the time of David, when he was faced with Absalom's rebellion: "David then made his way up the Mount of Olives, weeping as he went, his head covered and his feet bare." (2 *S* 15:30). The sites of interest here are: the Place of Ascension, the Pater Noster Church, Dominus Flevit Church, the Russian Orthodox convent and church of St Mary Magdalene, the Church of All Nations and Garden of Gethsemane, Tomb of the Virgin Mary and the Grotto of the Apostles. This is a good half day's excursion, and my preference was to walk (or taxi!) to the top, starting with the Place of Ascension, and then work on down.

CHAPEL OF THE ASCENSION

I found this rather a sad, forlorn little place, quite at odds with what it purports to commemorate - the Ascension of Jesus into Heaven. That the Ascension happened on the Mount of Olives is quite clear, as immediately afterwards, the Apostles, "...from the

Mount of Olives, as is it is called, they went back to Jerusalem, a short distance away..." (*Ac* 1:12), although the exact site is unclear. The Chapel is a small octagonal, domed shrine, in a walled enclosure, that sits back from the main road, up some wide steps, next to a small mosque. The current owners are Muslim, and a small entrance fee is charged.

There was a church here at the end of the fourth century, built by a wealthy Roman lady. This was destroyed in 614 by the Persians. Soon after, Bishop Modestus erected a circular building, described as being open to the skies and with windows being brilliantly lit at night, so that it was visible from the City. The present structure is basically Crusader, and all that remains, of what was reported as an impressive shrine with formerly an outer colonnaded cloister, is this octagon of slender arches and columns. The cupola was added by the Muslims when it came into their possession following the defeat of the Crusaders. It retains its Christian commemorative connection though, as the Muslims also believe and accept the Ascension of Jesus.

The fine 12th century Crusader marble capitals supported by the columns, with their elaborately entwined and deeply cut foliage, two with fantastic animal motifs, are worthy of admiration. Inside the minute Chapel is a *mihrab* (Muslim prayer niche) in the

Chapel of the Ascension.

south wall, and on the floor, in an asymmetrically placed frame, a rock with an indentation described as Christ's footprint. The Christian churches are permitted to celebrate Mass at the Feast of the Ascension, the metal rings high up on the outer walls being used to support a protective canopy. This is probably a place of curiosity rather than an inspiring holy site, and I got more from a visit to a nearby café, talking with the knowledgeable and hospitable Palestinian proprietor and his grandson, all of us rather circumspectly lamenting past, present and future! Behind the Chapel, and prominent on the skyline, is the Russian Church of the Ascension, of which opening times are very limited, check with the Christian Information Centre.

Here, pray (discretely) the Second Glorious Mystery of the Rosary - the Ascension, or alternatively at the Church of the Pater Noster (below).

THE CHURCH OF THE PATER NOSTER

A very short distance from the Ascension Chapel is the Church of Pater Noster. It is the home of the French Carmelite sisters, and commemorates the place where Jesus taught the Apostles the Lord's Prayer. Constantine ordered a church to be built here, over a cave (Eleona), as he did two other churches over caves in the Holy Land - the Holy Sepulchre and Bethlehem. It was noted by Eusebius and the Bordeaux Pilgrim as being dedicated to the Disciples and the Ascension. The site followed the familiar pattern of destruction and rebuilding; the former Crusader church lay in ruins for many hundreds of years, the ruins being occupied by Muslims.

In 1868 the Princess de la Tour d'Auvergne bought the land and built the present convent. An appeal to build a new church was launched by the French in 1918, work started in 1920, but funding ran out, and today one sees the unfinished building open to the elements. So apart from the convent and the rather plain, careworn but humble convent church, it is a strange mix of ancient and modern ruins. But as you wander up and down and through these ruins and cloisters you will see on the various walls, versions of the Our Father in over 60 languages of the world - note the small spelling mistake in the English! It is a peaceful place to wander and meditate the Lord's Prayer, and also the Ascension. There is a well stocked shop manned (or wo-manned!) by cheerful volunteers.

Meditation

Surely there are few of us, if we dwelt on the thought, but would feel it a privilege to use, as we do (for instance in the Lord's Prayer), the very petitions which Christ spoke. He gave the prayer and used it. His apostles used it; all the saints ever since have used it. When we use it we seem to join company with them. Who does not think himself brought nearer to any celebrated man in history, by seeing his house, or his furniture, or his handwriting, or the very books that were his? Thus the Lord's Prayer brings us nearer to Christ, and to his disciples in every age. No wonder then, that, in past times good men thought this form of prayer so sacred, that it seemed to them impossible to say it too often, as if some special grace went with the use of it. Nor can we use it too often; it contains in itself a sort of plea for Christ's listening to us; we cannot, so that we keep our thoughts fixed on its petitions, and use our minds as well as our lips when we repeat it. And what is true of the Lord's Prayer is in its measure true of most of those prayers which our Church teaches us to use. It is true of the Psalms also, and of the Creed; all of which have become sacred, from the memory of the saints departed who have used them, and whom we hope one day to meet in heaven.

(*Venerable John Henry Newman*)

DOMINUS FLEVIT

This lovely little modern church, owned by the Franciscans, further down the hill from the Pater Noster church, is for me one of the pilgrimage high points, not only on the Mount of Olives, but of Jerusalem as well. The church, in the shape of a tear drop commemorates when Jesus wept over Jerusalem, "As he drew near and came in sight of the city he shed tears over it.." (*Lk* 19:41). This was an ancient burial site (1600-1300 BC, and 1-4th century) as witnessed by the small tomb complex on the right immediately you enter the grounds. There was a 5th century monastery here, a chapel in the 14th century, superseded by a 17th century mosque. The Franciscans built a chapel in 1891, and the present church, designed by the Italian architect, Antonio Barluzzi, was built in 1955 over the remains of the earlier Byzantine monastery chapel.

It is set in quite extensive shrubbed and flower-bedded grounds, in a tranquil setting, and one with the most stunning and commanding view over the Old City. Here, one can meditate and pray, sitting quietly on the terrace outside the church. It has a distinct curved, bonnet-shaped dome, topped by a tall lantern. The four external pillars at each corner of the church are crowned by slim, graceful vases in which tears are caught. To the left of the church entrance are well-preserved mosaics from the floor of the Byzantine monastery's wine press, decorated with different types of fruit.

Inside, the church is high, light, airy, simple and peaceful. A most poignant view of the Old City is framed by the wide, arched, 'chalice-and-Host' window directly behind the altar, prominent through which is the distinct golden dome of the Dome of the Rock. This poignancy is even more accentuated, when during Mass and seeing this view, the call to prayer of the muezzins ring clearly out from the Old City. Notice at the back of the church the apse of an earlier church facing east rather than west, and the mosaics from this church incorporated on the modern flooring. One of the other lovely little whimsical touches is the mosaic on the altar-front of a hen with a halo gathering her chicks under her wings, "How often have I longed to gather your children together, as a hen gathers her brood under her wings, and you refused!" (*Lk* 13:34).

Meditation

Lord Jesus Christ,
today we share your tears
for the cities of the world;
- still we have not loved the things
that make for peace.

We weep for the divided cities:

Dominus Flevit - scene of Old Jerusalem through the 'chalice window'.

where brother fights with brother,
where anger feeds on hatred,
where prejudice blinds the eyes of compassion,
and even religion divides,
where children are taught to hate,
and old men relish ancient wrongs.

We weep for the cities of oppression:
where iron law imprisons freedom,
where thought is curbed and conscience stifled,
where the questioning spirit is called a traitor,
where art and civilising truth grow barren,
and each must think in manner as his neighbour.

We weep for the cities of poverty:
where children live, but die too soon,
where eager hands can find no work,
where hunger rules and aid is short,
where mothers clutch uncomprehending young,
and where the little we do, we fail to do.
We weep for our cities, and for ourselves;
We have not learned the things that make for peace.

Lord, Turn tears to love,
and love to work.
Turn work to justice,
and all that makes for peace.
(*Donald Hilton, Prayers for the Church Community,
National Christian Education Council*)

On your way down the steep, narrow road you will
pass, on your right, the Russian Orthodox Church of St
Mary Magdalene at Gethsemane. This very beautiful
church, with its seven recently re-gilded golden domes
and yellow stonework, is prominent on the Mount of
Olives. Opening times are quite limited (check with
the Christian Information Centre) but it is well worth a
visit, if opening coincides with your passing by. You
will also pass the extensive Jewish cemetery, where
every observant Jew would wish to be interred, within
the shadow of the Temple across the valley.

The order in which you visit the last three venues
will entirely be down to you, but if time and energy
are running short my recommendation is to
concentrate your efforts on the Church of All Nations
set within the Garden of Gethsemane.

CHURCH OF ALL NATIONS
AND GARDEN OF GETHSEMANE

This rather unusual and striking twelve-domed
church, belied from the front view by its conventional,
classical pillared and porticoed façade, is set in the
small, lovingly tended garden of what is left of the
ancient olive grove of the Garden of Gethsemane.
Here, Jesus suffered His agony before being betrayed
and led off to His trial and death. It is known as the

Church of the Agony. There is the inevitable speculation as to the age of the olive trees - they certainly are hundreds of years old, but although claims are made, they are unlikely to have been growing in Jesus' time. Although they are set in this neat, benign, bright be-flowered garden, invariably bathed in golden sunlight, their dark, gnarled, twisted and stunted trunks do bring to mind an atmosphere of a suffering of long ago.

The atmosphere inside the Church certainly, and deliberately, conveys this. On entering, you will be struck by the low light level effected by the purple glazing and the sombre interior, all invoking the ambience of Gethsemane on that Thursday night of agony. One's eye immediately falls upon the sanctuary and altar area: it is all of a piece, beautifully composed, and well worth meditating over what it portrays. The large, bowled apse is covered with a most striking and powerful depiction of the Agony. In this expansive and dramatic mosaic, Jesus is shown as a small lonely, solitary figure, slumped in despair on the rock; but high above, we can see an angel - protecting Him, praying over Him.

The tabernacle is set in the curved, amber marbled wall below, in a prominent, carved eight-pointed star. The altar stone is supported by a dramatic carved stone chalice. In front of the altar is the bedrock on

Garden of Gethsemane - ancient olive trees.

which, according to tradition, Jesus prayed in His agony. Encircling the rock is an iron wreath, a crown of thorns. In the centre of three sides is a pair of thorn birds in front of a communion cup, symbolising those faithful souls who want to share in the cup of Christ's Passion. At the near corners, a silver dove, trapped by the thorns, symbolising our entanglement in the thorns of life. The wreath is a gift from Australia. The mosaics in the side apses show the Kiss of Judas and the Arrest of Jesus.

In the wider church, one can view the Byzantine mosaic flooring, and the incorporation of Byzantine and Crusader foundations and coursings from the earlier churches on this site. This church was designed by the ubiquitous Antonio Barluzzi, and built in 1924, with a charming blend of Western and Middle Eastern architecture. It is called All Nations in acknowledgement of those countries who donated to the cost of building. If you crane your neck to look up at the domes above, you will see the flags and emblems of these countries embellished on them, including England and Ireland.

The Agony in the Garden

"He then left to make his way as usual to the Mount of Olives, with the disciples following. When he reached the place he said to them, 'Pray not to

Church of All Nations - sanctuary.

*be put to the test.' Then he withdrew from them,
about a stone's throw away, and knelt down and
prayed. 'Father,' he said, 'if you are willing, take
this cup away from me. Nevertheless, let your will
be done, not mine.' Then an angel appeared to
him, coming from heaven to give him strength. In
his anguish he prayed more earnestly and his
sweat fell to the ground like great drops of
blood."* (*Lk* 22:39-44)

Meditation

The will of God. That's what rules the world and
moves the stars, what converts the nations, what
brings to life and brings triumph out of death. The
will of God raised up Abraham, our father in faith;
it called Moses, inspired David, prepared Mary,
sustained Joseph, made Christ incarnate and
demanded his sacrifice; this it was that founded the
Church. And it is God's will still to continue the
work of redemption until the end of time. It will
call people to enter one by one into the visible
body of the Church when the time is ripe after
having belonged to his invisible soul through their
good intentions and good will. Whether you are on
the sand worshipping, or at the teacher's desk in
the classroom, what does it matter as long as you

are doing the will of God? And if the will of God urges you to seek out the poor, to give up all you possess, or to leave for distant lands, what does the rest matter? Or if it calls you to found a family, or take on a job in a city, why should you have any doubts? 'His will is our peace,' says Dante. And perhaps that is the expression which best brings into focus our deep dependence on God.

(*Carlo Carretto*)

Prayer

Father, help us to understand that Your will is that 'all be saved'. For this, You sent Your only Son, in which He gave His perfect obedience: to perfectly fulfil your saving will. We, humbly pray, Almighty God, that you unite our will with that of Your Son after the example of the ancient prophets, the Blessed Virgin Mary and all the saints. We beseech You that this loving plan be fully realised on earth as it already is in heaven. It is through our prayers that we seek discernment as to what is Your will, and we beseech for the steadfastness, courage and fortitude to follow it.

Here, also can be prayed the First Sorrowful Mystery of the Rosary - the Agony in the Garden.

On leaving, notice the fine, intricate, bronze doors, resembling olive trees. As you step out of the Gardens you will notice a small gate just across the road opposite. Through here is a quiet continuation of the olive grove which is available for prearranged group visits.

To do justice to the front façade, one should view it from across the main road, opposite. Atop the Corinthian columns are the four Evangelists. The colourful and vibrant mosaic shows Jesus as Mediator between God and us, on whose behalf He gives His own Heart through the hands of an angel. On Jesus' right the powerful and the wise humbly bow before Him, submitting the shortcomings of their wisdom and strength; on His left are the 'poor in mind, body and spirit', who offer their poverty in hope and confidence. The motto underneath "...he offered up prayer and entreaty, with loud cries and with tears to the one who had the power to save him from death, and winning a hearing by his reverence, he learnt obedience, Son though he was, through his sufferings" (*Heb* 5:7, 8). On the summit, the Cross surmounts a globe, and is flanked by two stags.

GROTTO OF THE APOSTLES

Diagonally across the road, next door to the Tomb of Mary in a sunken courtyard, is the Grotto of the Apostles, or the Cave of the Olive Press; it is also in the custodianship of the Franciscans. It is a quiet little haven, tastefully presented and well cared for. Tradition has it, as reported by Eusebius of Caesaria (circa 330) and others, that this is the place where Jesus used to come with the Apostles and pray at night when he was in Jerusalem, "All day long he would be in the temple teaching, but he would spend the night in the open on the hill called the Mount of Olives" (*Lk* 21:37). This is where he left the Apostles before His Agony in the Garden, "Then he withdrew from them about a stone's throw away..." (*Lk* 22:41), and where they slept whilst Jesus prayed.

There are fragments of evidence that there was a place of worship here in Byzantine times (mosaic at the back) and the Crusader period. Having lost ownership of the Tomb of Mary, next door, the Feast of the Assumption is formally celebrated here by Western Christians on 15th August. There are three small altars, each with a mural above - the Betrayal by Judas and the Assumption on the two side altars. Above the principal altar is the Evening Prayer of Jesus, which radiates such reverence from those who kneel before Him, and such a peaceful, powerful atmosphere of prayer shining from Jesus, as to move me quite profoundly. Notice under the altar, the two sleeping Apostles.

TOMB OF THE VIRGIN MARY

The last visit of this little pilgrimage sequence is to the Tomb of the Virgin Mary, also known as the Church of the Assumption. This crypt is all that remains of an upper church, built in the 6th century which 'surpassed the lower for grandeur', being destroyed as with so much else, by the Persians in 614. In 1130 the Benedictines rebuilt over the ruins, the Church of St Mary of Jehosophat, with an adjacent monastery, both of which were razed by Saladin circa 1187. Custodianship of the shrine passed from the Franciscans to the Eastern Orthodox churches in 1757. All that is left of this Crusader church is the rather unassuming plain, arched and pillared portal, which leads you down the 47 steps into the crypt.

Although the Church only refers to Our Lady's passing on with the words, 'when the course of her earthly life was finished' (Pius XII *Munificentisiumus Deus* 1950), there is a tradition in the early Church that Our Lady died (and was assumed into Heaven) in Jerusalem (see also the Church of the Dormition); this, in contrast to the more nebulous tradition that she later went to Ephesus in Turkey, with St John, and died there. It is this shrine that commemorates this - and it is all about her. The shrine is adorned in the Eastern manner, with swathes of hanging lamps,

ornate brocades, bright icons, and bare light bulbs.
With smoke-blackened ceiling, pervading aroma of
incense, and hushed atmosphere, it is a dark and
mysterious place. As you descend the wide stairs you
may notice two side chapels: on the left a chapel to St
Joseph, and on the right, to Mary's parents, Ss
Joachim and Anne (see also St Anne's church).

At the bottom, on the right, it is Mary's tomb that
dominates. It is fronted by an Eastern altar, richly
embellished with brocades, icons, candles and
pictures. Behind is the tomb, brightly lit from inside,
containing the remnants of a bench arcosolium tomb
probably dating from the 1st century. The edicule
encloses the bare rock of the natural tomb, much as in
Jesus' Tomb at the Holy Sepulchre. This early
Christian shrine is likely to have been part of the
burial vault of the family of Mary. The other altars in
the apses belong to the Armenians, Greeks and the
Ethiopians. There is a small Muslim *mihrab* (prayer
niche) indicating the direction of Mecca, south of the
tomb, in recognition of a once joint ownership with
the Muslims, and the fact that they too are still
permitted to pray there, venerating Mary.

❧ MOUNT ZION ❧

This is the area in the south west of Old Jerusalem, both inside and outside the present City walls, although in Jesus' time the whole area was enclosed within the City walls. Our area of interest today, is immediately outside, just south of the Zion Gate. Grouped closely together is the Cenacle (Upper Room), the Tomb of David and the Dormition Abbey, and, ten minutes' walk, just down the hill, the Church of St Peter in Gallicantu; by my reckoning, these two churches being the most striking in the Holy Land.

This area was reckoned by Constantine, by virtue of the tradition of the Last Supper being held here, to warrant building the fourth of his great churches in the Holy Land, along with the Holy Sepulchre, the Nativity, and the Eleona, now the Pater Noster. This church was known as *Hagia Zion* - Holy Zion, and was called the Mother of the Churches. The name Zion possibly meaning in Hebrew *sayon*, dry place, or in Arabic *sahwa*, mountainous ridge. In the Bible it is taken to be the holy mountain of Jerusalem; the dwelling place of God in the Temple, and the symbol of His presence. It is first mentioned in the Old Testament in 2 *S* 5:7, "But David captured the citadel of Zion, that is the City of David". Since then, Zion assumed the poetic and allegorical concept of being the Heavenly Place, particularly in the Psalms, and in many subsequent writings and hymns.

Also in this area is Caiaphas' house, where Jesus was taken and imprisoned, and where Peter betrayed Jesus three times. Here also is said to be the place where the Holy Spirit descended on Our Lady and the Apostles at Pentecost, and the house where Mary lived and died.

Following the cycle of building and destruction over the centuries, there has been a succession of churches built in and around these sites, with changing ownership between Christians, Muslims and latterly, Jews. There are indications that the Hagia Zion was extensive, as fragments from excavations showed that it covered the whole area of the Dormition Abbey, the Upper Room and the Tomb of David.

DORMITION ABBEY

The *Dormitio Sanctae Mariae* with its sturdy circular tower, grey, conical dome, and the tall, adjacent bell tower is a handsome, striking, modern church that dominates the Jerusalem skyline. It is sometimes mistaken for the Holy Sepulchre. The land was given by the Turks to their ally, William II of Prussia, who presented it to the German Catholic Society of the Holy

Land in 1898. The church was built between 1901 and
1910 in the Romanesque style. It is in the care of
German speaking Benedictine monks, and is the
responsibility of the Bishop of Cologne. It still bears
the scars of battle from the recent Israeli and Arab
wars, where for twenty years it stood in no-man's-land,
between the warring factions.

The four, square external towers embracing the
church belie the fact that inside it is completely
circular. It is spacious and lofty, with plain, bare pale
stone walls. There are no windows at the lower level.
Natural light is admitted high up through the modern
stained glass windows that pierce the barrel of the
dome. There are pillared and arched recesses at the
second level; the arched recesses at ground level
provide exquisitely mosaiced and marbled side
chapels. The middle one to the right is dedicated to St
Willibald, born in Wessex, and the first known
English pilgrim to come to the Holy Land in the 8th
century, who later became the Bishop of Eichstatt
(Franconia, in southern Germany).

The large sanctuary apse presents a golden
mosaic of the Madonna and Child in Byzantine,
iconic style. Below are eight Old Testament
prophets who foretold the coming of the Messiah.
The floor, often partially obscured by chairs, is an
intricate mosaic of concentric circles, depicting the

Basilica of the Dormition.

spreading of the Word through time and space, from the Trinitarian God, through the prophets of the Old Testament to the Evangelists of the New, and the twelve Apostles. The penultimate circle shows the months of the year in the signs of the Zodiac, the whole finally surrounded by the Latin quotation from *Proverbs* 8:23-25:

"From everlasting, I was firmly set, / from the beginning, before the earth came into being. / The deep was not, when I was born, / nor were the springs with their abounding waters. / Before the mountains were settled, / before the hills, I came to birth."

The church has lovely acoustics, often being the venue for concerts, and visiting when the fine modern organ is being played is a treat.

Crypt of the Dormition

Stairs at the back lead down to the crypt, which is in the form of a wide, circular, pillared hall with ambulatories. In the centre is a fine Beuronesque (after the form of art in Beuron Abbey, southern Germany) life-sized statue of the sleeping Virgin, carved from cherry wood and ivory. She is surrounded by a low, pink marble wall, on which six

Dormition Abbey - the Crypt.

intricately carved columns support a domed, mosaic cupola. The mosaic shows Jesus ready to receive His Mother into Heaven, and is surrounded by six women of the Old Testament: Eve, Miriam, Jael, Judith, Ruth and Esther. Around the crypt are six very distinctive side altars donated by various countries, from the stairs, working clockwise: United States, Brazil, Venezuela, Hungary, Austria, and a very unusual one from the Ivory Coast.

Leading off the crypt is the small main altar under a handsome apse showing Our Lady and the Apostles receiving the Holy Spirit at Pentecost. To the left a small Blessed Sacrament chapel, and to the right a miniature encaged Pieta, strewn with photos and messages of loved ones - each one telling a story, known only to God and their family, but over which we can also pray. This discreet sacred space is ideal to step away from the pilgrim mainstream for a few quiet moments.

All in all, this is a graceful, dignified, beautiful place to ponder something somehow overlooked by our Western Church minds - the Dormition. It is thrilling to sit quietly in the crypt, watching groups from many countries coming and going, many singing beautiful, evocative tunes and harmonies to Our Lady.

The vision of the woman and the dragon

"Now a great sign appeared in heaven: a woman robed with the sun, standing on the moon, and on her head a crown of twelve stars. She was pregnant, and in labour, crying aloud in the pangs of childbirth. Then a second sign appeared in the sky: there was a huge red dragon with seven heads and ten horns, and each of the seven heads crowned with a coronet. Its tail swept a third of the stars from the sky and hurled them to the ground, and the dragon stopped at the front of the woman as she was at the point of giving birth, so that he could eat the child as soon as it was born. The woman was delivered of a boy, the son who was to rule all the nations with an iron sceptre, and the child was taken straight up to God and to his throne, while the woman escaped into the desert, where God had prepared a place for her to be looked after for twelve hundred and sixty days. Then I heard a voice shout from heaven, 'Salvation and power and empire for ever have been won by our God, and all authority for his Christ, now that the accuser, who accused our brothers day and night before our God, has been brought down.'"
(*Rv* 12:1-6,10).

Meditation

For if he has blessed his saints with the whole
kingdom of heaven, if he opened paradise to a
thief with a single word, how much more would
he have been eager to welcome the one who made
him a home in her womb - the one whom he had
created, whom he had formed, from whom he
became flesh, as he willed. His purpose was that
the power of the Prince of Evil should be
destroyed through her by whom he had deceived
us.....For if, when he saw his disciples
discouraged by his passion, Jesus said to them, 'I
go to prepare a place for you' (*Jn* 14:2), how
much more will he have prepared a place for the
one who begot him - all the more so, as she had
all the more right of access to him! So the
immaculate body of the all-holy one, and her pure
soul, in which God took delight, were taken up to
heaven with an escort of angels. For if she had
received nourishment from angels in the Lord's
temple, while she was still a child, how much
more could she be served by the powers on high
after she had become herself the Lord's temple!
(*Bishop Theoteknos of Jericho, 7th century*)

Prayer of Protection

We fly to thy protection, O holy Mother of God.
Despise not our petitions in our necessities,
but deliver us always from all dangers
O glorious and blessed Virgin.

Here, also pray the Fourth Glorious Mystery - the
Assumption of Our Lady into Heaven. It may also be
appropriate to pray the Fifth Glorious Mystery - the
Crowning of Our Lady as Queen of Heaven and earth.

Above ground again, there is a well stocked and
extensive gift shop, and a quality café with toilets.

THE UPPER ROOM (CENACLE)

The place where the Last Supper is commemorated is
sited in a glorious hotch-potch of buildings which
neatly sums up Jerusalem's confused past! It is at
first floor level, the entrance being up some stairs
from the courtyard of what was an old pilgrim
hospice, then an Ottoman house and also part of a
Jewish *yeshiva* (academy). This is one of those points
along the pilgrim route where it can be said with total
certainty that this is not the original upper chamber,
nor is it likely to be the exact location. Other sources

place the Last Supper on the ground floor in what is now named the Tomb of David.

So, we have to stay with the upper room - a 'typical' 12th/14th century Gothic chamber so familiar in many European churches. There is also no obvious point of focus commemorating the Last Supper, or indeed Pentecost, but it is a fine room worth examining, as again it displays rather confused credentials!

The hall was part of the southern gallery in the upper level of the Crusader church of St Mary of Zion. The columns and carved 12th century Gothic capitals support a fine groined, roof vaulting. It is plain, white-walled, flag-stoned, dignified. There are traces of 14th century painted heraldry on the wall to the right of the door. If there is any focal point, it is on the south wall, being a handsome carved 16th century *mihrab*, flanked by two restored Ottoman coloured glass windows, and to its right an Arabic inscription on the wall prohibiting public prayer, all reflecting the period of ownership by the Muslims from the 16th century. Of specific Christian interest is the small, plain white dome in a corner and above some stairs, supported by a delicate marble column, of which the capital displays a fine example of carving by a Crusader mason. The carving depicts a mother pelican plucking her breast to bring forth blood on which her young are feeding -

symbol of Christian sacrifice, seen frequently in early churches but not often understood.

Pope John Paul II celebrated Mass here during his visit to the Holy Land in 2000, from where he signed and issued the Jubilee Year Letter to Priests for Holy Thursday. Ownership of the Upper Room was formally transferred to the Catholic Church after this visit, in exchange for a church in Toledo, Spain, which had originally been a synagogue.

The Institution of the Eucharist

"Then he took bread, and when he had given thanks, he broke it and gave it to them, saying, 'This is my body given for you; do this in remembrance of me.' He did the same with the cup after supper, and said, 'This cup is the New Covenant in my blood poured out for you'."
(*Lk* 22:19,20).

Meditation

The Church was born of the paschal mystery. For this very reason the Eucharist, which is in an outstanding way the sacrament of the paschal mystery, stands at the centre of the Church's life. This is already clear from the earliest images of the Church found in the Acts of the Apostles: 'They devoted themselves to the Apostles' teaching and fellowship, to the breaking of bread and prayers (2:42). The 'breaking of bread' refers to the Eucharist. Two thousand years later, we continue to relive that primordial image of the Church. At every celebration of the Eucharist, we are spiritually brought back to the paschal Triduum: to the events of the evening of Holy Thursday, to the Last Supper and to what followed it. The institution of the Eucharist sacramentally anticipated the events which were about to take place....In the humble signs of bread and wine, changed into his body and blood, Christ walks beside us as our strength and our food for the journey, and he enables us to become, for everyone, witnesses of hope. If, in the presence of this mystery, reason experiences its limits, the heart, enlightened by the grace of the Holy Spirit, clearly sees the response that is demanded, and bows low in adoration and unbounded love. (*Pope John Paul II*)

Prayer - Anima Christi

Soul of Christ, be my sanctification.
Body of Christ, be my salvation.
Blood of Christ, fill all my veins.
Water of Christ's side, wash out my stains.
Passion of Christ, my comfort be.

O good Jesu, listen to me.
In Thy wounds I fain would hide,
Ne'er to be parted from Thy side,
Guard me, should the foe assail me.
Bid me come to Thee above,
With Thy saints to sing Thy love,
World without end. Amen.

Here, pray also the Third Glorious Mystery of the Rosary - the Descent of the Holy Spirit, and, the Fifth Mystery of Light - the Institution of the Eucharist.

Whether permitted or not, I did find some stairs leading up to the flat roof, giving fine views of Old Jerusalem and the Kidron Valley.

THE TOMB OF DAVID

The Tomb of David is on the ground floor in the same building complex as the Upper Room. There is no archaeological or historical evidence that David is interred here, or indeed in the other places that have been suggested - Mount Ophel in Jerusalem or Bethlehem (cf 1 *K* 2:10). History does not recount how and why this tomb came to be placed here: the first century historian Josephus mentions it, and the

Crusaders, through their misunderstanding of exactly where Zion was, continued to place it here. Behind the tomb is the apse of the 1st century Christian house church on Mt Zion, one of the most important survivals from the time of Christ. It is also thought to have been part of Constantine's 4th century *Hagia Zion*. Again, this site has variously been in the hands of Christians, Muslims and now Jews. Today, it is a Jewish holy place of some significance. Entrance is through an antechamber, where women and men are directed separately. Men are required to cover their heads with prayer caps (*kippahs*), which are available.

I did not really know what to make of this place, particularly when one thinks of the grandeur and splendour of the tombs of our own great kings. It is in a relatively small, not particularly well appointed, space. The long sarcophagus, extending through the partition into the women's section, is bedecked with a weighty velvet cloth. On top rest silver crowns that once topped Torah scrolls, some saved from the Holocaust.

David is one of the towering figures of the Old Testament. In recognition of this, and our Old Testament heritage, we aught to spend some time here, at this place of tangible connection, pondering those roots that go down so deep, starting with the thoughts given by the Catechism, opposite.

David

"David is par excellence the king 'after God's own heart', the shepherd who prays for his people and prays in their name. His submission to the will of God, his praise and his repentance, will be a model for the prayer of the people. His prayer, the Prayer of God's Anointed, is a faithful adherence to the divine promise and expresses a loving and joyful trust in God, the only King and Lord. In the Psalms, David, inspired by the Holy Spirit, is the first prophet of Jewish and Christian prayer. The prayer of Christ, the true Messiah and Son of David, will reveal and fulfil the meaning of this prayer" (CCC 2579).

David's prayer

"Now, Yahweh God, may the promise which you have made for your servant and for his family stand firm forever as you have said, so that your name will be exalted forever and people will say, 'Israel's God is Yahweh Sabaoth.' Your servant David's dynasty will be secure before you, since you, Yahweh Sabaoth, the God of Israel, have disclosed to your servant, 'I am going to build you a dynasty.' Hence your servant has ventured to offer this prayer to you. Yes, Lord Yahweh, you

are God indeed, your words are true and you have
made this generous promise to your servant. What
is more you have deigned to bless your servant's
dynasty, so that it may remain for ever before you;
for you, Lord Yahweh, have spoken; and may your
servant's dynasty be blessed with your blessing for
ever" (2 *S* 7:25-29).

ST PETER IN GALLICANTU

The last of our stops in the Mount Zion area is the
church of St Peter in Gallicantu. This is also one of the
places where there is conjecture over whether or not this
was the site of Caiaphas' palace. The title of the church
commemorates Peter's thrice denial of Jesus: *'galli
cantu'* meaning 'cock crow' in Latin. The conjecture is
based on the fact that someone in Caiaphas' position as
High Priest would have had his residence in a far more
commanding and prestigious location on Mount Zion. A
site owned by the Armenians near the Dormition
Abbey, as yet un-excavated, is a contender. However,
excavations round the Gallicantu site give evidence that
it was a household of some importance, as it had its own
water cistern, corn store, domestic quarters and
underground cellars; artefacts such as weights and
measures as used by priests in the Temple, and a door

St Peter in Gallicantu.

lintel with the word *Korban*, Hebrew for 'sin offering', as well as other objects from the Second Temple period, have come to light.

There is also no clear history of any preceding churches on this site. There are fragmentary remains that indicate the presence of a 6th century Armenian monastery, the possibility of a 9th century Greek church of St Peter, where 'the glorious apostle wept', this church apparently surviving the 11th century upheavals, as pilgrims were recorded visiting a church of 'St Peter in Gallicantu' in the 12th century, but this was apparently in ruins in the 14th century. There are records of pilgrims visiting a cave in this area subsequently, but by the mid 15th century, there is no surviving trace. The present church was built in 1928-32 by the French Assumptionist Fathers.

Today's church

As you approach the church and convent complex from above, you see below you a rather squat, 'clumpy' building, topped by a grey dome and cross, atop which is a golden cockerel, with a small, arched and grey-capped bell tower. At the bottom of the car park, and before you turn left for the church there is a viewing balcony which gives you a spectacular and 'reverse view' from when you were on the Mount of Olives looking towards the Old City. Here you can

see the whole of the Kidron Valley and the Mount of
Olives, with all the familiar landmarks such as
Dominus Flevit and St Mary Magdalene. It also gives
a striking impression of the extent of the Jewish
cemetery that you passed on your way down to the
Church of All Nations and Gethsemane - the whole
hillside appears dazzling white in the sun, etched with
the sharp lines and shadows of the many thousands of
raised graves on the terraced hillside.

I found this whole place an absolute treat, and
worth lingering over. Entry to the church is through
the impressive bronze doors depicting Jesus
foretelling Peter's denial, "I tell you, Peter, by the
time the cock crows today you will have denied three
times that you know me" (*Lk* 22:34). The external
squat appearance is explained inside - the church is in
the shape of a symmetrical cross. And when looking
round you see a multi-apsed church, all beautifully
linking with each other. One can follow the
progression, from the main apse - high and barrel
vaulted, to the two smaller apses each side of the main
altar, to the large, shallow transept and rear apses,
right down to the eight slender apses in the eight
corners of the church, the two rear ones cleverly used
as confessionals.

The walls and dome are a swathe of vibrant, modern
mosaics, showing scenes of Jesus' life - the one above

the main altar with Jesus standing before Caiaphas.
There is a clean, wooden lattice screening at the lower
level all round the church. The dome is striking and
beautiful. It is in the form of a multi-coloured stained
glass cross, light pouring through it. There is a simple,
patterned, inlaid marble floor. A fascinating church in
its details and mosaics - it is bound to distract, and
needs time to take it all in and appreciate it!

The Court Room

Further surprises await you as you proceed down the
levels of the church complex. At the next level is the
'Court Room' - in fact a spacious, light chapel, which
most effectively incorporates the bare rock of the
hillside as one of its 'walls'. Although square in shape
it is given a 'rounded' effect with the arches over and
meeting in the centre of the ceiling. There is a plain,
square apse, of which the centre fresco, in iconic
style, shows a distraught Peter weeping, "And he went
outside and wept bitterly" (*Lk* 22:62). Just to the left
front of the sanctuary is a sizeable glassed and railed
observation port looking down deep into the dungeon
complex below. Trellised and latticed windows of
amber, lemon and blue give a soft, warm light to the
chapel. At the far side and up some stairs to a
mezzanine level is a lovely intimate, glassed-in
Blessed Sacrament side chapel. Here is the place to

pray without distraction before Our Lord, present in the handsome brass tented and illuminated red, stained-glass tabernacle.

Peter's denials

"Meanwhile Peter was sitting outside in the courtyard, and a servant girl came up to him saying, 'You too were with Jesus the Galilean.' But he denied it in front of them all. 'I do not know what you are talking about,' he said. When he went out to the gateway another servant girl saw him and said to the other people there, 'This man was with Jesus the Nazarene.' And again, with an oath, he denied it, 'I do not know the man.' A little later the bystanders came up to Peter, 'You are certainly one of them too! Why, your accent gives you away.' Then he started cursing and swearing, 'I do not know the man.' And at once the cock crowed, and Peter remembered what Jesus had said, 'Before the cock crows you will have disowned me three times.'" (Mt 26:69-75)

Meditation

Having fled from the garden, Peter skulks to a fire where he is asked three times if he knows Jesus Christ. And Peter denies him. But he cannot deny the truth. Peter knows Jesus' mercy. It moves him to compunction, to tears. And reinstated, Peter will strengthen his brothers and sisters as a priest. For without the priesthood we would forget God. Without the priesthood the sacraments would dissipate into sentiment. At the fire, Peter forgets himself. But mercy reminds him of his truest identity: he is a priest, another Christ, an instrument of mercy whose whole life is holy and ordered to grace...fully devoted - not to self - but to the Body of Christ, the Church. The night before he dies, Jesus, the only Priest, gives us the gift of the priesthood to be our unending source of consecration. For the priest is commanded to offer the Eucharist 'in memory of' Jesus. It is the priesthood that enables us to remember Jesus as he insists on being remembered. It is the priesthood that keeps us from denying the truth of God and remaking Him according to our own image, whim and inclination. United in the tears of Peter the priest, we are drawn anew, with courage and conviction, through the tyranny of this sordid night, to 'hold fast to God's grace, through which we may offer worship acceptable to him in reverence and awe. For our God is a consuming fire.' (cf *Heb* 12:28-29)

(*Fr PJ Cameron OP*)

Prayer

Dear Jesus, in our prayer to you at this place where Peter fell prey to human weakness on that sordid night, we remember particularly our own parish priest, as well as the priests of our diocese, our Bishop, and Your Chief Shepherd, the Pope: they too are all prey to human weakness. Strengthen them, we beseech you by Your saving grace and Your supreme example - because on the night you gave yourself to the Father, you were human too. Give them the courage to weep bitterly when they deny you, and wash them through with Your saving and renewing mercy as they atone. Help us too, to support and be loyal to our parish priest, to let him know of our love for him, as we pledge to give him spiritual succour through our own prayers and support. We ask this in Your most Holy Name. Amen.

Dungeons

Carrying on down below this chapel is the dungeon complex, which is well presented and self explanatory, and worth exploring, bearing in mind the possibilities of Jesus' imprisonment the night before He was crucified. On the upper level is the prison described in the Acts of the Apostles, into

which the Apostles were thrown. Below is a single
cell, into which a prisoner could be lowered by
means of a rope. This was possibly the fate of Jesus
in the hours after His trial. This is shown by the
mosaic on the side of the church from which you
approach, of Jesus being hauled up by his shoulders
(cf *Jr* 38:10-13). In the cell one should also note the
seven faint red Byzantine crosses and four carved
into the rock face, which are said to date back to the
4th century; the black ones having been added at a
later date. Here one can read and meditate the
Prisoner's Psalm which is provided for visiting
pilgrims - *Psalm* 88.

To round off your visit, leave the dungeon
complex at the lower level, where outside there is a
quite extensive terraced, shaded garden with good
views of the Kidron Valley, below. In these grounds
there are archaeological excavations, some
sculptures and bas-reliefs. What is of greatest
interest though, are the wide and ancient steps that
go up past the church - the Maccabee steps - which
are the original steps in Jesus' time, used by the
local folk to climb up from the Kidron Valley to
Mount Zion. On these steps Jesus walked in His
comings and goings between the Mount of Olives
and the Temple.

"...in the footsteps of the Master...' - the Macabee Steps.

This is a lovely place to sit in the sun, in peace, and look down on the valley below, listening to the muted sounds as they float up, contemplating that it may well have looked very similar in Jesus' time, with the untidy jumble of flat-roofed houses (despite the satellite dishes!) - and yes, you will hear a cockerel crow!

On the higher terrace, above the church, is a pleasant coffee house and well stocked shop.

❧ OTHER PLACES ❧

This chapter describes venues that are not necessarily conveniently linked either in theme or geography, but all well worth a visit in their own right, starting with those in and around Old Jerusalem, and then going further a field to Bethphage, Bethany and Emmaus.

ST ANNE'S AND THE POOL OF BETHESDA

"Now in Jerusalem, next to the Sheep Pool there is a pool called Bethesda in Hebrew, which has five porticoes; and under these were crowds of sick people, blind, lame, paralysed." (Jn 5:2-3).

These pools, and St Anne's Church, are to be found just inside Lion's Gate, inside the Muslim quarter. A visit here can be tied in with doing the Stations of the Cross. This site was used as a reservoir in the 8th century BC, feeding the First Jewish Temple. In Roman times the pools had a reputation for their therapeutic properties, and hence the gathering of the sick. As recorded in John's Gospel the sick were "...waiting for the water to move; for at intervals the angel of the Lord came down into the pool, and the water was disturbed, and the first person to enter the water after this disturbance was cured of any ailment from which he was suffering". Origen, in the 3rd century, describes the four porticoes round the sides, with the fifth across the central rock-cut division of the pools.

Detailed excavations were only carried out since 1956 and revealed the remains of a sizeable 5th century Byzantine church, the Church of the Paralytic, of which a section was built over the pools. This church was destroyed by the Persians in 614, and in the 12th century the Crusaders built, along with the adjacent church of St Anne, a small chapel on the remains of the northern nave of the Byzantine church. This can be very clearly seen and shows a very distinct example of one church being built on the other, below. The ruins can seem rather a bewildering jumble, and will need sorting out with the display boards that are close at hand, or leaflets from the entry kiosk. The ruins present a fascinating unfolding story of these healing pools in very early times.

St Anne's

If one is allowed to have a favourite church in the Holy Land, mine would be St Anne's. This plain, rather austere Crusader church has a marvellous graciousness and dignity about it - solid on the outside, plain beauty inside. Rather like some 'liturgical' churches of

Pools of Bethesda (foreground) and the Church of St Anne.

enclosed religious orders, it is devoid of any familiar devotional displays - no Stations of the Cross, no statues, no pictures, mosaics or icons, no stained glass windows. Light comes in through the small diamond shaped apertures in the high, arched windows. The only exception is a beautiful white marble statue, at the back of the church, of St Anne, with Our Lady as a young girl, at her side.

The site tells the usual story of destruction and regeneration. Tradition has it that Our Lady's parents, Joachim and Anne, had their house here. A Byzantine church was built in the 5th century, destroyed in the 7th, rebuilt soon after, with the present church being erected by the Crusaders in the 12th century. A convent was also built here for Benedictine nuns, endowed by the Crusader King Baldwin I, into which he placed his wife, Arda!

When Saladin captured Jerusalem in 1187 the church was turned into a Muslim religious school (*madrasa*), and his inscription in Arabic is evident on the tympanum above the main door and probably saved the building from any further destruction by Muslims in ensuing conflicts. Even into the 17th century, Christians regarded this place as the home of Joachim and Anne. The Franciscans were allowed to say Mass in the crypt on the feasts of the Immaculate Conception and the Nativity. After this period the place was gradually abandoned on the grounds that it was haunted, and this beautiful building ended up as a stable for the Turkish Governor's cavalry. In 1856 the church and grounds were handed to Napoleon III by the Turks in thanks for help given to them by the French during the Crimean war. There is a story that it was previously offered to Queen Victoria, who turned it down in favour of Cyprus! Then in a ruinous state, it was restored in the 1860s, and is in the ownership and care of the White Fathers.

St Anne's 'secret'

St Anne's also has a marvellous, mischievous 'secret', which is intriguing, humorous and ingenious! When I asked the priest-in-charge who was showing me round if there was one special thing he would like to tell me about his church, of which he was so obviously proud, he said, with a bit of a twinkle, "Yes, there is - it must be one of the most asymmetrical churches in the world." I looked blank. He then proceeded to show me what he meant, and it took a bit of getting used to, but once spotted there was no going back! Initially when you go in, you get the impression of total symmetry and harmony - this is what we expect going in to a building like this, and this is what our eye tells us.

But if you start looking carefully, there is actually very little symmetry in the detail. Opposite columns do not match in design, there is no 'mirroring' of sides, windows are all different sizes, buttresses differ in thickness and height, stair edges do not line up from where they start to where they finish. The mischief is that this is all beautifully and carefully designed. My guide's claim was that there was not a single 'straight line' in the place, and he gleefully recounted the biannual visit of the very serious architectural students who come and check and marvel, claiming that the building should have fallen down soon after it was built!

The acoustics in this church are sublime, and listening to visiting groups who can really sing, is transcendent. Below, there is a 5th century crypt which commemorates Our Lady and her parents; two side altars are placed in earlier Roman caves.

Although St Anne's and the pools are busy at times, their setting in a tranquil courtyard garden, with palm trees, conifers, orange trees and quiet corners here and there, is one of the havens of peace in this busy, noisy town. It was only the bird song that was deafening! This should also be noted as one of the few decent loo stops on the pilgrim route in Old Jerusalem!

ECCE HOMO CONVENT

Whilst the Convent and all that goes with it is on the route of, and closely associated with, the Way of the Cross, my recommendation is that you treat a visit here as separate, so as not to detract from both; if you have time you could visit St Anne's Church just a short distance away, then *Ecce Homo*, and then start the Stations of the Cross, virtually next door, in the Franciscan Monastery of the Flagellation.

The Convent was founded in 1855 by a French/Jewish convert, Father Alfonse Ratisbone for the Sisters of Zion. It is built on what was part of the Roman Antonia barracks and fortress, which Herod the Great dedicated to Mark Antony. This was one of two places where the Roman governor, or praetor, would stay when visiting Jerusalem from his headquarters at Caesarea by the sea. By tradition this was therefore held to be the area in which Jesus was condemned to death by Pilate. By the 16th century, the so called *Ecce Homo* arch, spanning the *Via Dolorosa*, was revered as the place where Pilate displayed the scourged prisoner to the crowds baying for his blood, with the words '*ecce homo*' - 'behold the man' (*Jn* 19:5). The actual archway is in fact dated slightly later than Jesus' time, being attributed to Herod Agrippa I (41-44), having been built as the eastern city gate.

The Convent complex contains a series of fascinating features to wander round and explore at leisure. This includes a vast underground Roman reservoir system, known as the Struthion Pool, as well as the *Lithostrotos* (Greek for pavement), a section of Roman pavement, which is referred to in John's Gospel: "...Pilate had Jesus brought out, and seated him on the chair of judgement at a place called the Pavement, in Hebrew Gabatha" (*Jn* 19:13). Although laid a century later in the construction of *Aelia Capitolina*, there is the reasonable assumption that these huge flags were recycled from earlier times, and over which Jesus may well have walked. It is fascinating to note the grooves cut in the slabs to drain away rain water, the striations to help horses grip with their hooves, and the holes, which were probably used to support street lanterns. In this dramatically displayed area there is an altar, on which Mass can be celebrated, and nearby, carved into a flagstone, are the features of a dice game played by Roman soldiers known as the King's Game, at which, on occasions, the prize for winning was the prisoner's robes (*Mt* 27:27-30).

Convent chapel

The Convent also has a charming chapel, a quiet place off the *Via Dolorosa* to pray and meditate. It is a narrow, tall, arched and triple-domed church,

Via Dolorosa - Ecce Homo arch.

plain, unadorned - and like so many convent chapels, redolent with its deep silence of prayer and grace. The sanctuary is dramatically simple, with its huge jumbled blockwork wall and arch of ancient bricks, fronted by a simple stone altar. Above, through a separate, precisely built arch, is a golden sunburst mosaic apse centred with an intricately designed cross, into which is woven a crown of thorns. The most striking and ingenious feature, but not glaringly obvious, is the continuation of the *Ecce Homo* arch from outside the *Via Dolorosa*, its left hand span arcing through the outer wall of the chapel, and joining with the smaller sanctuary arch inside, of which it is a part. Immediately by the inner entrance to the chapel is a beautiful statue of Christ the King, radiating dignity and silent suffering.

Here, pray the Second Sorrowful Mystery of the Rosary - the Scourging at the Pillar; also the Third Sorrowful Mystery - the Crowning with Thorns.

As you leave the Convent and turn on to the Via Dolorosa, pray also the Fourth Sorrowful Mystery - Jesus Carries His Cross.

THE GARDEN TOMB

Immediately north of the Old City, a short walk from Damascus Gate, is the Garden Tomb, also sometimes known as 'Gordon's Calvary', another oasis of peace and tranquility in amongst the noisy and dusty, fumy, city bustle. This ancient burial site was discovered around 1867, but it was General Gordon of Khartoum, in 1883, when ironically, a period of British military activity in the Middle East reawakened interest in Holy places and pilgrimages, who was convinced that this place was the site of Calvary. He based this on the facts of its antiquity, it being outside the (present) city walls, and nearby, a rock face resembling the features of a skull - Golgotha. This rock face can quite clearly be seen, just beyond and above the bus station, when walking the Old City ramparts past the Damascus Gate. The story goes that he telegraphed Queen Victoria proclaiming that he had found the site of the true Calvary, to which he received a gracious thanks, but adding that she intended to maintain the tradition 'first established by our cousin Helena'.

However, neither archaeology nor tradition support this claim. The skull-like caves do not appear in drawings of the place as late as the 17th century. There is evidence that quarrying and tunnelling was carried out in the 1st century, and of it being a burial site by the 8/9th centuries. However, pictorially, and atmospherically, it does present a far more idealistic setting than the cluttered urban surroundings of the Holy Sepulchre and its rather gloomy atmosphere. It is a delightful place, with green, shady gardens, immaculately kept, meandering paths, and lots of little quiet places dotted around. The centrepiece is the small, square tomb, which you enter through an oblong aperture in the rock face. Inside the plain, unadorned rock chamber are three much worn projecting benches with troughs. This is such a contrast to the Tomb at the Holy Sepulchre. I found it quiet, dignified, unsupervised, unhurried, calm and simple - a charming, peaceful place in which to pause and reflect.

Although it can be quite busy at times, it is not chaotic, being extremely efficiently run and organised. Although interdenominational, it is much favoured by Protestant and Evangelical groups, who understandably may not be able to face up to the pomp and circumstance of the setting and demeanour of the older denominations who lay claim to the Holy Sepulchre! Opening hours are limited, there is a well stocked shop and decent toilets!

The Garden Tomb.

Prayer for Christian Unity

Almighty Lord, no one can lay any foundation
other than the one that has been laid. That
foundation is Jesus Christ. We admit that we have
not been able to finish building on this foundation
in such a way that we may become the dwelling
place of God. We have sometimes even been the
cause of its ruin. Even if our work should be lost,
save us, Lord, and give us a fresh chance to work
for unity. Create in us an ardent longing for the
unity of your Church and enable us to work
towards it. Amen.

FRANCISCAN CHURCH OF ST SAVIOUR

Whilst not on the mainstream pilgrim trail, the church
of St Saviour in the north western corner of the Old
City, in the Christian Quarter, is well worth a visit.
The church and associated monastery is the hub of the
Franciscan administration and custody of the *Santa
Terra*, the Catholic sites in the Holy Land. From here,
and indeed round the City and in the other holy
places, you will spot Franciscans from every country
in the world, pursuing their mission of maintenance of
the *Terra Sancta* and care for the Palestinian people.
The tall, elegant bell tower dominates this part of the

Old City. The church is 'modern', having been completed in 1885, paid for by the Austrian Emperor.

It is a three aisled Basilica, with a barrel vaulted ceiling, very 'European' in style, giving one quite a strange feeling of displacement, having been exposed to all the contrasting sites on one's pilgrim journey in the Holy Land. The church serves not only the monastery, but is also the Parish Church to the Palestinian Catholics in Jerusalem. One of the highlights of my pilgrimage was to come to early morning Mass being celebrated by a Franciscan Palestinian priest in Arabic! Having worked many years in the Middle East in a completely Muslim context, this was a very moving and unique experience, hearing the Liturgy in Arabic, and realising that the Allah being praised was the God of the Trinity!

LATIN PATRIARCHATE

Amidst all the high profile holy places in Jerusalem, it is well worth casting a thought, and a prayer, to the workaday life of the Church that goes on round the world in its dioceses - Jerusalem being no exception. Just a few minutes' walk from St Saviour's is the seat of the Latin Patriarch of Jerusalem. This is the title given to the Roman Catholic Archbishop of Jerusalem, who has jurisdiction over all Catholics in

Israel and Palestine, thus is currently the only Eastern patriarchal title to be assigned to a Latin Rite Bishop. The present incumbent, Archbishop Michel Sabah, is the first Palestinian to fill this See.

His cathedral is styled as a co-cathedral (with the Holy Sepulchre), and is dedicated to the Holy Name of Jesus. It was completed in 1872 in the Gothic style. It has an impressive ceiling mural depicting Old Testament people and scenes, through to New Testament and early Saints. There is a copy of the well known statue of St Peter, whose original is in St Peter's, Rome. An impressive picture of the Circumcision to the left of the altar was donated by Napoleon III; on close examination it turns out to be a very skilfully close woven tapestry. More details are available on their website *www.lpj.org.*

THE TEMPLE

"Stand at the gate of the Temple of Yahweh and there proclaim this message. Say, 'Listen to the word of Yahweh, all you of Judah who come in by these gates to worship Yahweh. Yahweh Sabaoth, the God of Israel says this: Amend your behaviour and your actions and I will let you stay in this place." (Jr 7:2, 4).

The Temple features prominently in the Old Testament. Indeed during the centuries of its existence (1006-586 BC), the First Temple was regarded by the Biblical authors as the only legitimate shrine of God, although other shrines existed in the northern kingdom of Israel. Most of the kings of Judah were crowned in its court; it was where the great festivals were celebrated with copious animal sacrifice. The Second Temple, is featured frequently in the Gospels, and was still the prime focus for the Jews in Jesus' day: he was presented there forty days after his birth as a first born male, 'to be consecrated to the Lord' (*Lk* 2:23); he asked questions of the elders and scribes when he was a young boy, and he frequently visited when he was in Jerusalem during the period of his ministry. Having driven the moneylenders out of the Temple, Jesus' riposte to the angry Jews was: "'Destroy this Temple, and in three days I will raise it up.' The Jews replied, 'It has taken forty six years to build this Temple: are you going to raise it up again in three days?' But he was speaking of the Temple that was his body..." (*Jn* 2:19-21). The Jews maintained, through this, that he had invoked some kind of curse against the Temple, and was therefore a legitimate charge of blasphemy against him at his trial.

The First Temple was built by David's son, Solomon, in 961 BC: 'I propose, then, to build a temple for the name of Yahweh my God, in accordance with what Yahweh told my father David,' (1 *K* 5:19). Chapter 6 contains a detailed account of its construction and furnishings. Here the Ark of the Covenant, symbol of God's protection since the times of the Exodus, was solemnly installed. The Temple was completely destroyed by the Babylonians in 586 BC; the disappearance of the Ark of the Covenant at that time has led to much legendary speculation, popular even today.

The Second Temple was rebuilt on the same site, but not on the same scale, by Zerubbabel, 537-515 BC, after the Babylonian Exile. This temple was completely replaced by Herod the Great starting in 20 BC, and was completed not long before its destruction during the first Jewish uprising by Titus in 70 AD. It was a magnificent edifice, the scale of which is evident from the massive platform on which it sat, that still exists as the Muslim Haram al-Sharif (Noble Sanctuary) on which the Dome of the Rock and Al Aqsa mosque are placed.

Ruin

It sat in ruins for many decades; early writers record that Hadrian set up pagan statues on the site as part of the development of his Roman capital city *Aelia Capitolina*, which were subsequently dismantled by

Constantine. Generally Christian reaction to the site of the ruined Jewish Temple was ambivalent: it was a holy site in Christian terms, as Jesus had been presented in it, and frequently visited and taught there. But on the other hand, this desolation starkly portrayed Jesus' prophecy that 'not one stone should be left upon another', and was clearly a demonstration of the failure and impotence of the Old Covenant compared with the visible advance of the New, as evidenced by Constantine's splendid new Church of the Resurrection - the *Anastasis* - the new Holy of Holies, and the many other churches and communities springing up all over the Roman Empire. And because of this huge effort and focus on the site of Calvary, the Temple Mount was therefore largely disregarded during Byzantine times for development or use as a Christian site.

Muslim holy site

After the Arab conquest in 638 it became the focus of Muslim veneration and development - it having been recognised and accepted as a sacred site for Muslims. Construction of the Al Aqsa Mosque began in c. 639, and the Dome of the Rock in 691. Destruction and rebuilding followed earthquakes and fire. During the time of the Crusaders the Dome was converted into a Christian church and Al Aqsa became the headquarters of the Templar Order (hence the name of the Order). After the defeat of the Crusaders in 1187 the site was reclaimed by the Muslims, and redevelopment continued. Today the gleaming golden Dome of the Rock is the enduring iconic image of Jerusalem. With this most holy site having been in possession of all three faiths at some time, it sums up all that is Jerusalem - beauty belying turbulence.

Temple Mount Today

I sensed desolation wandering round this huge flat expanse, punctuated with its impressive holy buildings; a lack of joy or vibrancy, so unlike the rest of Old Jerusalem. There were few people around at the time, and maybe the atmosphere is different during worship time, when unbelievers are not allowed. There was also a substantial Israeli police and military presence, giving an air of unreality: Jews maintaining civil order on what is their holiest site, one which the Orthodox Jew will not set foot upon until the coming of the Messiah, but to the Muslims it is also the second holiest site, after Mecca.

The south east corner of the site is known as the Pinnacle of the Temple which represents the high point to which Satan took Jesus during his temptation, 'Then he led him to Jerusalem and set him on the parapet of the Temple, 'If you are Son of God,' he said to him, 'throw yourself down from here...' (*Lk* 4:9). You may be able to walk up onto the battlements and enjoy spectacular views of the Kidron Valley from this point.

The Dome of the Rock and the Al Aqsa Mosque are very beautiful inside, and well worth a visit. Opening days and times and access points to the mosques are limited: check with the Christian Information Centre. Do not take any overtly 'holy objects' with you - my Bible was impounded by Israeli security at their entry check point for the duration of my visit.

> Here (or by the Western Wall), one can pray (very discretely) the Fourth Joyful Mystery of the Rosary - The Presentation of Jesus in the Temple, and the Fifth Joyful Mystery - the Finding of the Child Jesus in the Temple.

The Western Wall

I have to say, with the bluntness of someone who is at times somewhat over-curious, that the Western (or Wailing) Wall is a most fascinating place to visit. Here one observes the Jewish Faith at its most fervent, and at its most concentrated - in dress, demeanour and spiritual atmosphere. Here one can experience tangible vibrancy and energy. This place is the scene of intense, and continuous worship, generating a sense of passion, and even desperation. To the Jews it portends an enduring symbol of hope.

Here is Judaism at its most Orthodox - the distinctive Hasidic dress: the men with their wide-brimmed black hats, or the *spidic streimel* - large circular fur trimmed hat; flowing, long black coats, black trousers - or sometimes black stockings, their *peyot* - the long bouncing, hair ringlets, swinging in front of their face, sometimes tucked behind their ears. Here you will see and hear the faithful at prayer, earnestly poring over the long Talmudic scrolls, embracing the Wall, rocking to and fro in prayer - imploring, beseeching the Divine Presence (*Shechina*) that they believe soars above it. It is very moving, and if to our Western sensitivities too demonstrative, it is certainly exemplary in its commitment and intention.

A visitor, Loti, was moved to write when he visited in 1895: "Against the wall of the Temple, against the last debris of its past splendour, are the Lamentations of Jeremiah which they all repeat.... 'Because of the Temple which is destroyed,' cries the Rabbi. 'We sit alone and weep!' replies the crowd. 'Because of our walls which are fallen,' 'We sit alone and we weep!' 'Because of our majesty which has passed, because of our great men who are no longer alive.' 'We sit alone and weep!'"

Wailing Wall.

The Wall is actually the massive foundation stones of the podium to Solomon's and Herod's Temples, some of the huge, pale stones weighing up to twenty tons. Following the destruction of the Temple, the Western Wall gradually and intermittently became the focus for Jewish pilgrimage. As a place of lamentation it became known as the 'Wailing' Wall - even during times of Muslim occupation. Whilst the space available for the limited amount of pilgrims was adequate in the earlier centuries, it became more constricted as numbers increased and as buildings encroached on the land beneath it - many of them belonging to Muslims, including a mosque. Ironically in 1948, when the State of Israel declared its independence, the Western Wall was inaccessible from Israel, and it was not until the Israeli occupation of the 1967 War that they gained direct access to this area.

Subsequently the whole area below the wall was cleared, to create the extensive plaza that exists today. I certainly felt free to pray there, going and kneeling at the Wall, placing my petition in the large cracks in the Wall, joining those tens of thousands of other written pleas and petitions over the ages. Whilst doing so, I could not help but reflect on this extraordinary juxtaposition of this most holy Jewish place - the last remnant of their holiest place - being at the foot of the mighty Muslim shrine that took its place, directly above.

**Prayer placed by Pope John Paul II in the
Western Wall**

God of our fathers,
you chose Abraham and his descendants
to bring your Name to the Nations:
we are deeply saddened by the behaviour of those
who in the course of history
have caused these children of yours to suffer,
and asking your forgiveness
we wish to commit ourselves
to genuine brotherhood
with the people of the Covenant.
We ask this through Christ our Lord.

BETHPHAGE

*"When they were near Jerusalem, and had come to
Bethphage on the Mount of Olives, then Jesus sent
two disciples...."* (Mt 21:1).

Bethphage is the small village just over the Mount of
Olives from Jerusalem. It is walkable from the Pater
Noster Church, and given extra time could be
included in the trip described in the Chapter on the
Mount of Olives. Here, Jesus, by tradition, mounted
the donkey that took him into Jerusalem on that first
Palm Sunday. The Franciscan Monastery Church,

built in 1883 on a 12th century Crusader site, commemorates this. Access is through the monastery gate. In the church, protected by a wrought iron grille, is a large stone 'mounting' block denoting this event. The many paintings in the church, mostly restored in 1950, portray the events of Palm Sunday; the church ceiling is covered with an attractive painting of sprays of flowers. From vantage points round here there are stunning views across to Bethlehem and the Judaean wilderness, and on a clear day it is possible to make out the Jordan valley, and on the other side, the Mountains of Moab.

BETHANY

"Six days before the Passover, Jesus went to Bethany, where Lazarus was, whom he had raised from the dead. They gave a dinner for him there; Martha waited on them and Lazarus was among those at table. Mary brought in a pound of very costly ointment, pure nard, and with it anointed the feet of Jesus, wiping them with her hair;..." (*Jn* 12: 1-3).

Although only 4 kms from Jerusalem, Bethany suffers the isolation of being cut off from the natural route through to Bethphage and hence on to

Jerusalem by the Israeli Separation Barrier. It is therefore not all that convenient in terms of geography, and a detour has to be made to get to the check point that gives access. This place, more so than Bethlehem, is possibly in danger of becoming bypassed and neglected through this isolation. In crossing this area, the Barrier cut through three Catholic properties.

Bethany was 'home from home' for Jesus, where he would often stay whilst in Jerusalem with his close and trusted friends Martha, Mary and their brother, Lazarus. At this place today is a modern Franciscan Church dedicated to St Lazarus, built over the traditional home of Lazarus, Mary and Martha. The church was designed by Barluzzi and completed in 1954, and is in the care of the Franciscans. It stands over the ruins of three previous churches: a 4th century church, about which St. Jerome testified: "Bethany is a village at the second milestone from *Aelia* [Jerusalem], on the slope of the Mount of Olives, where the Saviour raised Lazarus to life, to which event the church now built there bears witness". This church was replaced after an earthquake by a 5/6th century, larger church, which in turn was destroyed by the Persians in the 7th century. Over those ruins a large Benedictine convent was built by the Crusaders in the 12 century, which incorporated the Tomb of Lazarus, stretching as far as the present Greek Orthodox church, and on to the prominent ruined tower which marked the western boundary of the Convent.

From the outside, today's church presents an austere image - unadorned, stark and blank-walled. Presumably Barluzzi's design intention was to portray the mausoleum which was to have been Lazarus' Tomb. This theme is carried inside by the rather gloomy, dark interior from the windowless lower level. However, this is effectively contrasted by the only source of natural light that floods in high up from the dome, symbolising the light of the Resurrection, and further emphasised by the inscription from *Jn* 11:25 round the cupola, "Anyone who believes in me, even though that person dies, will live, and whoever lives and believes in me will never die". The dome mosaics are laid as flowering blossoms, interspersed with flames and flying doves, symbolising the sweetness and warmth of those faithful souls ascending to heaven. The church is in the form of a symmetrical Greek cross; on the apse wall a mosaic of the Resurrected Jesus proclaiming, "I am the Resurrection and the Life" (*Jn* 11:25); on the other three walls mosaics of Jesus with Martha and Mary, Jesus raising Lazarus, and Jesus dining with Simon the Leper.

Tomb of Lazarus

Just up the hill from the church is the Tomb where by tradition Lazarus was interred, and from where Jesus raised him from the dead: "...he cried in a loud voice, 'Lazarus come out!'. The dead man came out, his feet and hands bound with strips of material, and a cloth over his face. Jesus said to them, 'Unbind him, let him go free'." (*Jn* 11:43, 44). The Tomb is on the site of a 16th century mosque, with its prominent minaret, which was built on the ruins of the old Benedictine Convent. The site is in the care of Muslims, who also venerate Lazarus as a prophet. The current entrance was constructed by the Franciscans in the 16th century to avoid having to enter via the mosque. Twenty six steps lead down a curving, uneven stairway to a further 3 shallow steps which go down into the small inner vestibule, the entrance to which one has to stoop to gain access.

A bit further up the road from the Tomb is the 1964 red-domed Greek Orthodox Church, with stepped bell tower topped by a delicate pillared dome, dedicated to Simon the Leper. Behind that, the ruins of the once imposing west tower of the old Benedictine Convent, with its base of some massive Herodian stone blocks.

EMMAUS

*"Now that very same day, two of them were on
their way to a village called Emmaus, seven miles
from Jerusalem, and they were talking together
about all that had happened. And it happened that
as they were talking together and discussing it,
Jesus himself came up and walked by their side;
but their eyes were prevented from recognising
him."* (*Lk* 24:13-16).

The location of Emmaus, the village that Cleopas and
his fellow disciple were walking to when the Lord
appeared to them after the Resurrection, has never
been truly pinned down. There are three main
contenders, which are briefly listed below:

Amwas

Corruption of Arabic word 'Emmaus', 'hot springs'.
It is the oldest site linked with this event, but as it is
19 miles from Jerusalem it is the most unlikely
geographically, with the two disciples faced with a 38
mile return journey within the day. At this site are the
ruins of a sizeable 5th century Byzantine church, with
some evidence of later Crusader activity. The gates to
the site are often locked, and therefore can only be
viewed from a distance.

Abu Gosh

This village, is just off the main highway from Jerusalem to Tel Aviv, some 11 kms from Jerusalem. The Church of the Resurrection is in the tranquil, lush grounds of a French Benedictine Monastery. Although there are no credible sources identifying this site as Emmaus, it was celebrated by the Crusaders with the building of this diminutive, elegant Crusader church. Inside the airy, arched church are some original pictorial depictions of Emmaus; in the crypt is a spring dating back to Neolithic times. Dominating the village though, is the modern church of Our Lady of the Ark of the Covenant, whose tower is formed by a huge statue of the Madonna and Child. This church symbolises a lovely coming together of the Old and New Covenant: for here the Ark of the Covenant was stranded for many years before being taken by King David to Jerusalem in about 1000BC; today, this church celebrates Mary as the New Ark of the Covenant.

El Qubeibah

This was one of the sites identified by the Crusaders as a 'possible' for the location of Emmaus. It is 11 kms northwest of Jerusalem. On it stands the church of Cleopas, consecrated in 1902, having been built over a previous Crusader church. It is in the custody of the Franciscans. Within the grounds there is a section of excavated Roman road, linking Jerusalem with Caesarea, of which the conclusion is drawn that this is the road that Jesus walked with the two disciples. On the left of the nave, protected by glass and a wooden panel in the floor, are the remnants of what is claimed to be the house of Cleopas. This is a peaceful place with commanding views; from the balcony in the gardens one can see the distant foothills running down to the coast. Currently, it would appear to be the favoured site for Emmaus, as on Easter Monday many pilgrims come here to witness the 'blessing of the bread' by the Franciscan Custodian of the *Terra Sancta*.

❧ VIA DOLOROSA ❧

"If anyone wants to be a follower of mine, let him renounce himself and take up his cross and follow me." (*Mt* 16:24)

Stations of the Cross

Today's Fourteen Stations of the Way of the Cross thread a torturous path through the crowded, narrow streets and alleyways of the Old City. It was not defined in its present form until the 15th century and beyond, although devotions commemorating Jesus' Passion sequence have been carried out by Christians here in some form since early times. St Jerome in the 4th century records crowds of pilgrims from all countries who visited and prayed at these holy places. With descriptions starting to circulate throughout the Christian world, the ingenuity of some devotees led to a re-creation of these important shrines of Jerusalem in their own countries, allowing those who were unable to travel to the Middle East an opportunity to commemorate and reverence the Passion. A prime example of this was St Petronius, Bishop of Bologna, who in the 5th century built a series of connecting chapels representing the Jerusalem sites, at the monastery of San Stefano, to the extent that the monastery became known as *'Hierusalem'*.

These early devotions were the genesis of the current Tradition. In the early days there were many variations, of which one version included thirty five stopping points! It was only when the question of indulgences started to be considered that any consistent shape and form started to emerge. This was influenced largely by the Franciscans, not only in developing the Way in Jerusalem, but also as a universal format for use in churches round the world, employing the now familiar tableaux scenes. In 1731, Pope Clement XII extended indulgences to all churches who followed the devotion, fixing the number at fourteen. This was further refined in 1742 by Pope Benedict XIV, who further encouraged parish priests to equip their churches with the pictures or images of each individual Station.

Via Sacra

The earliest use of the word 'Stations' as applied to the stopping places on what was then called the *Via Sacra* in Jerusalem, emerges from the narrative of a 15th century English pilgrim, William Wey, who in 1462, described how pilgrims followed the route of Christ's journey to Calvary. Interestingly, in Wey's time there were also fourteen Stations, but only five of those corresponded with the ones in use today.

There is no doubt, though, about the significance that this devotion plays in the Catholic Church - of the remembrance and reliving of Jesus' journey to His suffering and death, conducted during Lent in every church throughout the world. This importance is further emphasised when the Pope conducts Stations on Good Friday at the Colosseum in Rome.

Via Dolorosa

Apart from this significant annual event in Rome, it is a great grace for those pilgrims who have the privilege of actually following the Way that Jesus struggled along in Jerusalem. Today's walking distance is about 900 metres, mainly uphill, through the uneven, cobbled steps of the Old City. The exact route in Jesus' day is not known in detail, other than the starting point at Fort Antonia, where He was condemned, to where He was crucified and entombed at Calvary, the present location of the Church of the Holy Sepulchre, which in those days was outside the City walls.

The Stations along today's *Via Dolorosa* come in all sorts of shapes and sizes - some in small chapels directly off the street, others just marks, plaques or symbols on the walls. You may have to keep your eyes peeled to spot them, or simply ask, as there is usually no lack of willing helpers! The last five Stations (X-XIV) are in the Church of the Holy Sepulchre. Unless you follow the Way very early in the day, do not count on it being a peaceful or particularly meditative journey, as essentially you are passing through the centre of a jostling Middle Eastern market town in full swing.

It also seems a bit hit and miss as to whether the chapels en route are open or available. Do not be daunted though. It is a fair bet that when Jesus passed along this route, it was just as busy and noisy; try to welcome this and include it all in your prayer as you progress. If you are without your map of Old Jerusalem (which can be obtained from the Christian Information Centre), fear not, there is no lack of eager salesmen ready to sell you their route leaflets at the start!

On Good Friday 2005, Pope John Paul II was fifteen days away from his death, and too ill to personally attend the *Via Crucis* at the Colosseum. He asked Cardinal Joseph Ratzinger, his successor and now Pope Benedict XVI, to write prayers and meditations for this occasion, which the Pope followed on television in his private chapel. In prefacing these Stations of the Cross, Ratzinger wrote, "Jesus himself interpreted for us the meaning of the 'Way of the Cross'; he taught us how to pray it and follow it: the Way of the Cross is the path of losing ourselves, the path of true love. On this path he has gone before us, on it he teaches us how to pray the Way of the Cross."

What follows is some background and descriptions of the Stations, with relevant Scripture passages to meditate on, in addition to your own devotions.

---

1 - Jesus is condemned to death

Just through Lion's Gate and past St Anne's church there is a modern and well defined gathering place for the Stations on the left, just off the street. A bit further on is the First Station. This is traditionally held in the courtyard of the Arab Omariye College, on the left. By its location as the former Fort Antonia, it represents where Jesus was condemned by Pilate, and mocked and scourged by the Roman soldiers. This is generally only accessible on Friday afternoons, when at 3pm the Franciscans gather, with those of the faithful who wish to follow the Way with them. The alternative, and more practical and appropriate venue at any other time, is either the Chapel of the Flagellation, or the Chapel of Condemnation, both in the courtyard of the Franciscan Monastery, on the right, just before the *Ecce Homo* arch and Convent, and now a Bible School.

The Chapel of Flagellation

This chapel is on the right as you enter the courtyard. It dates from 12th century and was redesigned and rebuilt by Antonio Barluzzi in 1927-29. It is a simple, single-aisled, pillared and vaulted chapel. There is a lovely gold-mosaiced dome over the altar, presenting a crown of thorns pierced with stars. Three stained glass windows also show: the scourging, Pilate washing his hands, and the freeing of Barabbas.

"Pilate said to them, "Then what should I do with Jesus who is called the Messiah? "All of them said, "Let him be crucified! " Then he asked, "Why, what evil has he done? "But they shouted all the more, "Let him be crucified! " So he released Barabbas for them; and after flogging Jesus, he handed him over to be crucified." (Mt 27:22-23,26)

2 - JESUS TAKES UP HIS CROSS

Whilst again the exact location of this Station is not specific it can be prayed either in the courtyard of the Monastery, or, in the Chapel of Condemnation, on the left of the courtyard.

The Chapel of Condemnation

This is an early 20th century chapel built on mediaeval foundations. It is a high, domed chapel with four beautiful pink pillars and daylight streaming in from the dome above; behind the altar is a striking and moving portrayal of Jesus being led from the Antonia Fortress to shoulder His Cross. At the back you will notice the enormous striated flagstones, the continuation of which are directly next door in the *Ecce Homo* Convent, about which more is described in the Section on *Ecce Homo* Convent. Outside, opposite the entrance, is a model of Jerusalem in the 1st century, showing Calvary outside the City walls.

"Then the soldiers of the governor took Jesus into the governor's headquarters, and they gathered the whole cohort around him. They stripped him and put a scarlet robe on him, and after twisting some thorns into a crown, they put it on his head. They put a reed in his right hand and knelt before him and mocked him, saying, "Hail, King of the Jews!" They spat on him, and took the reed and struck him on the head. After mocking him, they stripped him of the robe and put his own clothes on him. Then they led him away to crucify him." (Mt 27:27-31)

3 - JESUS FALLS FOR THE FIRST TIME

Having moved on down the *Via Dolorosa* and turned left, you will find this Station in, or by, a small chapel, on the left and through some blue metal gates, close to the busy junction of the *Via Dolorosa* and El Wad St. It is known as the Polish Chapel, as funding for its renovation in 1948 came from Polish soldiers who served in Palestine during the Second World War. It is owned by the Armenian Catholic Patriarchate. Above the arched entrance is a bas-relief of a defeated and exhausted Jesus, head bowed, as he collapses under the cruel weight of His physical and spiritual burden. This is rather a lovely, narrow and minute, three domed chapel. At the end is an evocative combined statue and mural of the fallen Jesus being lamented over by a host of angels.... "...a comforter who could revive me is far away" (*Lm* 1:16).

"Surely he has borne our griefs and carried our sorrows; yet we esteemed him stricken, smitten by God, and afflicted. But he was wounded for our transgressions, he was bruised for our iniquities; upon him was the chastisement that made us whole, and with his stripes we are healed. All we like sheep have gone astray; we have turned everyone to his own way; and the Lord has laid on him the iniquity of us all." (Is 53:4-6)

4 - JESUS MEETS HIS MOTHER

This Station is only a few yards further down, on the left, from the Third. Above a small arched doorway (which leads into an Armenian Catholic enclosure) with metal doors is a bas-relief bust of Jesus and Mary staring agonisingly and hopelessly into each other's eyes - Mary clutching Jesus' wrist in desperation. "All you who pass, look and see: is any sorrow like the sorrow that afflicts me?" (*Lm* 1:12)

"Simeon blessed them and said to Mary his mother: "Behold, this child is set for the fall and rising of many in Israel, and for a sign that is spoken against (and a sword will pierce through your own soul also), that thoughts out of many hearts may be revealed". And his mother kept all these things in her heart." (Lk 2:34-35, 51)

5 - Simon of Cyrene is forced to carry Jesus' Cross

Again, not far from the previous Station, on the corner of a street junction, is the Fifth Station. This will be recognised by the engraved lintel over a plain doorway set in pale brickwork, *'Simon Cyrenaeo Crux Imponitur'*, with a carved 'V' and 'ST' and Jerusalem crosses either side. The door leads into a small Franciscan chapel of plain yellow brickwork. Inside is a powerful bronze statue of Simon of Cyrene helping Jesus with His task.

"As they went out, they came upon a man from Cyrene, Simon by name; this man they compelled to carry his Cross. Jesus told his disciples, "If any man would come after me, let him deny himself and take up his cross and follow me." (Mt 27:32; 16:24)

6 - Veronica wipes the face of Jesus

This Station is further on up the same street as the Fifth, on the left. You will recognise it by its brown double wooden doors with black metal banding, and in the middle, the metalwork letters 'VI STATION'. In the shop next to it to the right, as often as not, the Little Sisters of Jesus are at work, and they will let you in to the chapel, as well as have a chat, where they proudly point out that Pope Paul VI stopped here during his visit in 1964.

The chapel is crypt-like with its candlelight and cool, vaulted stonework. The site is by tradition Veronica's house. It also has an association with a Byzantine church known as the 'House of Cosmas and Damian', after the 4th century martyrs, twin brothers and physicians, who tended the sick for no charge. The tradition is that Veronica, greatly moved by the suffering Jesus, took great courage for a woman in those times, by dashing free from the crowds, and attempted to comfort Jesus as best she could by wiping the blood and sweat that must have been blinding Him as He struggled up this street. She was rewarded by the imprint of His face appearing on her cloth (as her name implies in Greek, *verum*, true, *icon*, image). She is reputed to have taken the cloth to Rome and given it to Pope Clement I; it is lodged at St Peter's Rome, and several miracles have been attributed to it.

"You have said, "Seek my face". My heart says to you, "Your face, Lord, I do seek". Hide not your face from me. Turn not your servant away in anger, you who have been my help. Cast me not off, forsake me not, O God of my salvation." (Ps 27:8-9)

7 - JESUS FALLS FOR THE SECOND TIME

At the top of the street, at the 'T' junction, is the Seventh Station. Above a grilled window and door you should be able to see the Roman numerals 'VII'. Although often obscured by the clutter of the surrounding market stalls - the doors lead into a Franciscan chapel, which is normally open. This Station is geographically significant, because it marks what was the western boundary of the original City wall, out of which Jesus was led to Calvary, and it was included in the 14th century route. Scholars conclude that this was the location of the Judgement Gate, and where the sentences of death of those to be crucified were posted, as depicted by a very dramatic, and helpful, painting just inside the small narthex of the chapel. The chapel is brightly lit, and has pictures of Jesus falling, as well as a finely executed bronze.

"I am the man who has seen affliction under the rod of his wrath; he has driven and brought me into darkness without any light. He has blocked my way with hewn stones, he has made my paths crooked. He has made my teeth grind on gravel, and made me cower in ashes." (*Lm* 3:1-2, 9, 16)

8 - Jesus meets the women of Jerusalem

Off the busy main thoroughfare, up a narrow side street is the Eighth Station. This is the trickiest to spot, as it is only marked by a small Latin cross at eye level, on the left, on the wall of a Greek monastery; but it is only 30 or 40 metres from the Seventh. Around the Cross is carved the letters 'IC XC NIKA', translated as 'Jesus is victorious'. Its blackened appearance and small aperture at the bottom is explained by a lit candle sometimes being placed in it.

"Jesus turned to them and said, "Daughters of Jerusalem, do not weep for me, but weep for yourselves and for your children. For behold, the days are coming when they will say, 'Blessed are the barren, and the wombs that never bore, and the breasts that never gave suck!' Then they will begin to say to the mountains, 'Fall on us'; and to the hills, 'Cover us'. For if they do this when the wood is green, what will happen when it is dry?" (*Lk* 23:28-31).

9 - JESUS FALLS FOR THE THIRD TIME

A short retracing of the route is required, and then
turn right along the main alley away from the 7th
Station, keeping an eye out for some steps about 100
metres on the right, which will lead you up and
around to the Ninth Station. This is set within the
outer wall of, and within sight of the Holy Sepulchre,
reminding us that Jesus fell within sight of His
Calvary. It is marked by a worn upright pillar set in a
wall beside an archway straight ahead, that leads into
the Coptic Catholic Patriarchate.

> *"It is good for a man that he bear the yoke in his
> youth. Let him sit alone in silence when he has laid
> it on him; let him put his mouth in the dust - there
> may yet be hope; let him give his cheek to the
> smiter, and be filled with insults. For the Lord will
> not cast off for ever, but, though he cause grief, he
> will have compassion, according to the abundance
> of his steadfast love."* (Lm 3:27-32)

The remaining Stations are all within the Church of
the Holy Sepulchre. Entry can usually be made
immediately from the Ninth Station through the
doorway on the left to the Ethiopian rooftop
monastery, and then on down through their two

chapels into the Holy Sepulchre forecourt. If this route is closed, you will have to circumnavigate round to the main entrance to the church. There are minor variations as to where these Stations can be prayed, crowds and availability being one consideration, as well as your own choice and feeling. Detailed descriptions of these venues are given in the Chapter on the Holy Sepulchre.

10 - JESUS IS STRIPPED OF HIS GARMENTS

This Station can be conducted in the forecourt by the external stairs on the right of the main entrance leading up to a closed porch - but be warned this is also the place where the jolly group photos are taken! The alternative is in the Roman Catholic chapel of the Nailing to the Cross.

> *"And when they came to a place called Golgotha (which means the place of the skull), they offered him wine to drink, mingled with gall, but when he tasted it he would not drink it. And when they had crucified him, they divided his garments among them by casting lots; then they sat down and kept watch over him there."* (Mt 27:33-36)

11 - JESUS IS NAILED TO THE CROSS

In the Chapel of the Nailing to the Cross.

"And over his head they put the charge against him, which read, 'This is Jesus the King of the Jews'. Then two robbers were crucified with him, one on the right hand and one on the left. And those who passed by derided him, wagging their heads and saying, "You who would destroy the temple and build it in three days, save yourself! If you are the Son of God, come down from the Cross". So also the chief priests with the scribes and elders mocked him, saying, "He saved others; he cannot save himself. He is the King of Israel; let him come down now from the Cross and we will believe in him"." (*Mt* 27:37-42)

12 - JESUS DIES ON THE CROSS

In the Greek Orthodox Chapel of Calvary.

"Now from the sixth hour there was darkness all over the land until the ninth hour. And about the ninth hour Jesus cried with a loud voice, "Eli, Eli, lama sabachthani?" That is, "My God, my God, why have you forsaken me?" And some of the

bystanders hearing it said, "This man is calling Elijah". And one of them at once ran and took a sponge, filled it with vinegar, and put it on a reed, and gave it to him to drink. But the others said, "Wait, let us see whether Elijah will come to save him." And Jesus cried again with a loud voice and yielded up his spirit." (*Mt* 27:45-50)

13 - JESUS IS TAKEN DOWN FROM THE CROSS

Either by the Stabat Mater altar, at the front and between the two chapels, or on the ground floor, by the Stone of Anointing.

"When the centurion and those who were with him, keeping watch over Jesus, saw the earthquake and what took place, they were filled with awe, and said, "Truly this was the Son of God!" There were also many women there, looking on from afar, who had followed Jesus from Galilee, ministering to him." (*Mt* 27:54-55)

14 - Jesus is laid in the Tomb

In the vicinity of the Tomb.

"Joseph took the body, and wrapped it in a clean linen shroud, and laid it in his own new tomb, which he had hewn in the rock; and he rolled a great stone to the door of the tomb, and departed. Mary Magdalene and the other Mary were there, sitting opposite the sepulchre." (Mt 27:59-61)

The Passion

Whilst Egeria was in Jerusalem she made detailed observations of the liturgy in the Holy Sepulchre; as part of the good Friday devotions she noted:

"It is impressive to see the way all the people are moved by these [the Passion] readings, and how they mourn. You could hardly believe how every single one of them weeps during the three hours, old and young alike, because of the manner in which the Lord suffered for us. Then, when three o'clock comes, they have the reading from St John's Gospel about Jesus giving up the ghost, and, when that has been read, there is a prayer, and the dismissal."

❦ FINAL THOUGHTS ❦

Having travelled this Holy Land - whether by car, coach, foot or armchair - we will inevitably be left with impressions, emotions, memories, desires - some very clear - such as the Scriptures coming vividly alive as you gaze out on, or recall to mind, or imagine those holy places; others more nebulous, which you may still be trying to fathom.

But in some way the Lord will have revealed Himself, maybe obvious at the time, or, maybe latterly through hindsight and reflection; maybe striking, or maybe tenuous - through people, places, events, or thoughts.

Spiritually, you may have been inspired by those deeds and memories of the *past* which may in turn strengthen you and your Faith in the *present*.

Emotionally, you may have been moved by the *present*, having sensed the problems of this land and the plight of all its peoples - and with your prayers and support, be able to help them in their *future*.

And it may be, through all this, you will be called, or recalled, to make this pilgrimage, for the first time, or again. In the words of the Cardinal Archbishop of Westminster, Cormac Murphy-O'Connor, having returned from his Christmas 2006 visit to the Holy Land with the Archbishop of Canterbury and other church leaders, "Please, please, if you possibly can, go on pilgrimage to the Holy Land. It will be well worth it, not only for yourselves but also for the Christian community who live there."

For in human terms, what was real then, is real now - the blessings, the strife, the joy, the pain - to individuals, families, communities, nations - nothing changes.

In divine terms, what was real then is also real now. But far more than that. Although Jesus sacrificed His human life as part of the salvific plan, his Divinity lives on - it always has and always will: '*Heri, Hodie, Semper*': Yesterday, Today, Always. As human he 'proved' God's love for us, through the yesterdays of living, ministering and dying in this Land. But as a Divine Being He continues to show us His love *today*, and *always* will.

To reassure us of all this, He left us His Word; to feed us, He gifted us the Eucharist, both of which emanated from this Land, along with all those people who lived here: prophets, priests, kings, ordinary folk, Jew and Gentile. But He came not just for them - for he commanded the Apostles, all His followers throughout the ages - and us right now:

"I have made you a light to the nations,
So that my salvation may reach
The remotest parts of the earth" (Ac 13:47)

Jesus - God and Man

Closing Meditation

St Gregory Nazianzen, Bishop of Constantinople (379) and close friend of St Basil the Great, sums up the sublime paradox of Jesus the Man and Jesus the God in this lovely meditation on which to close this leg of your pilgrimage to the Holy Land. It expresses His humanity on earth as told in the New Testament and as testified to by the places you have visited. But it also tells of Jesus the Divine God, who is with us for eternity:

He was mortal, yet God;
of the race of David, yet the maker of Adam.
He wore flesh, yet was beyond bodily form.
He had a Mother, yet she was a Virgin.
He was circumscribed, yet had no limit.
The manger contained Him,
yet a star led on the Magi
who came bearing gifts and bent the knee.
He came to the contest as a mortal,
but as the unconquerable one
he vanquished the Tempter
in that threefold struggle.
He himself stood in need of food

but he fed many thousands of men
and turned water into wine.
He himself was baptised in the water
yet he washed away all our sins
while the thundering voice of the Spirit
proclaimed him Son of the Unoriginate One.
As mortal man he yielded to sleep,
but as God he hushed the sea.
His limbs were weary
yet he gave strength to the limbs
of paralysed men.
He prayed, but he it was who heard
the prayers of the poor.
He was sacrifice and celebrant,
sacrificial priest and God himself.
He offered blood to God to cleanse
the entire world.
The Cross lifted him up
but it was the trap that nailed sin fast.
And yet how can I speak of all his works?
He was numbered with the dead
but he rose up from the grave
and raised those dead long before.
Here at once is mortal poverty
And incorporeal riches.
Amen.

❧ THE HOLY LAND❧
A TIME LINE

Only the briefest sign posts to the long complicated history of this land can be given in a book such as this; a little more detail is given of the Christian era.

3000 BC - Canaanite Rule

1800 - Hebrew Patriarchs

1250 - Exodus from Egypt

1200-1000 - Judges

1000 - 931 - David and Solomon

960 - First Temple

930 - Schism between North and South

721 - Exile of North - Assyrian Rule

586 - Exile of South - Babylonian Rule

538 - Persian Rule - Return of Jewish exiles, Second Temple

332 - Alexander the Great - Hellenistic Period

167 - Macabee Rebellion

63 BC - 324 AD Roman period

63 BC - The Romans, under Pompey, conquer and annexe Palestine

37 BC - Herod the Great establishes Herodian dynasty, under the rule of Roman governors (one being Pontius Pilate 26-36AD). Temple of Jerusalem rebuilt.

4 BC - Birth of Jesus

27-30 AD - Ministry of Jesus and Crucifixion

70 AD - First Jewish Uprising against the Romans, suppressed by Titus, Jerusalem totally destroyed

132-135 - Second Jewish Uprising, crushed by Hadrian, causing the Jewish Diaspora (Dispersion). Roman capital *Aelia Capitolina* built over Jerusalem. Persecution of Jews and Christians continues under Roman rule

313 - After the Roman Emperor Constantine's conversion to Christianity, the Edict of Milan legitimises Christianity as the State religion, Palestine included within the Eastern Christian Roman Empire

324 - 634 Byzantine period

330 - Byzantine rule starts with Emperor Constantine, extensive building of churches throughout the Empire. Large scale pilgrimage to holy places, particularly in 5/6th centuries. Palestine a centre for monasticism; bitter conflict between Judaism and Christianity

614 - Widespread destruction from Persian (Sassanian) conquest, which was short-lived. Teachings of Muhammed being accepted throughout Arabia

632 - Death of Muhammed

634-1099 - Early Islamic period

634 - Arab nations embark on a series of conquests in the name of *jihad*

638 - Jerusalem falls to Caliph Umar I, beginning succession of Arab dynasties. Some tolerance to Christianity shown initially, but increasing persecution over time culminating in,

1009 - destruction of Church of the Holy Sepulchre in Jerusalem

1054 - Great Schism between Eastern and Western Churches

1099-1291 - Crusader period

1099 - Increasing threat to Christianity in the region generates Crusades from Western Europe, with establishment of Latin kingdom of Jerusalem. Many fine churches and fortresses built. Primacy of Western (Latin) Church re-established over control of holy sites. But Crusader occupation difficult to sustain, and in,

1187 - Moslem Prince, Saladin, under a united Muslim army, defeats Crusaders at the Horns of Hittin, and in

1291 - Last Crusader foothold in Acre, taken

1187-1917 - Later Islamic period *A long complex period where various Muslim dynasties conquered, ruled, succumbed:*

1169-1250 - The Ayyubid Dynasty, Egyptian, founded by Saladin. Mostly Sunni Muslims, tolerant to Judaism and Christianity

1250-1517 - The Mamluk Dynasties (Egypt), which fell to:

1517-1917 - The Ottoman Dynasty, under which the Eastern Church prospered over the Latin Church, and under

whom the Status Quo was established (see Introductory Chapter)

1920-1948 - British Mandate period

1917 - Defeat of the German and Ottoman armies by Arab and British armies, Balfour Declaration supporting a Jewish Homeland in Palestine 'without prejudice to non-Jewish population'

1922 - British mandate approved by League of Nations. Increasing hostility between Arabs and Jews over land and sovereignty, between Jews and British over occupation and immigration of Zionists, leads to,

1948 State of Israel and Palestinian Territories

1948 - End of Mandate. State of Israel declared, followed immediately by first Arab Israeli War, precipitating huge exodus of Palestinians

1948-1967 - Country partitioned under armistice agreement, and administered variously by

Israel, Jordan and Egypt. Mass immigration of Jews

1967 - Six Day War, occupation of West Bank, East Jerusalem, Sinai, Golan Heights by Israel. Jewish land appropriation, settlement and development increased and ongoing. Continuing tensions and instability

1973 - Yom Kippur War. Pre-emptive attack on Israel by Egypt and Syria; eventually repulsed by Israel with further territorial gains

1987 - First Palestinian *Intifada* (uprising) against Israeli control of Occupied Territories. Ended 1991

1993 - Oslo Accords, framework agreement for Palestinian self-rule in Occupied Territories. Israel and Vatican establish diplomatic relations

2000 - (March) Pope John Paul II's five day visit to Holy Land, where he stated he was 'deeply saddened by the hatred, acts of persecution and displays of anti-Semitism directed against the Jews by Christians at any time and in any place'.

2000 - (September) Second Palestinian (*Al Aqsa*) *Intifada*, sparked by Ariel Sharon's controversial visit to the Temple Mount

2004 - Withdrawal of Israeli settlers and military from Gaza Strip

≈ INDEX ≈

People

Places

Bibliography

The Holy Bible - The New Jerusalem Bible (Study Edition), Darton, Longman and Todd Ltd, London, 1994.

Catechism of the Catholic Church, Geoffrey Chapman, London, 1999.

BROWNRIGG, RONALD. *Come, See the Place*, Hodder & Stoughton, London, 1985.

CAMERON OP, FATHER PETER JOHN (Editor in Chief), *Magnificat (for some Meditations and prayers)*, New York, monthly.

DOROT, REUVEN (Editor). *Holy Land Journey*, DOKO, Yehuda, Israel, 1997.

DOYLE OFM, STEPHEN. *The Pilgrim's New Guide to the Holy Land* Michael Glazier, Wilmington, Delaware, 1987.

FOURE, CATHERINE (Editor) *The Holy Land*, Everyman Guides, London, 1995.

PRAG, KAY. *Israel and the Palestinian Territories*, Blue Guide, A&C Black, London, 2002.

RICHARDS, H. J. *Pilgrim to the Holy Land*, McCrimmons, Great Wakering, England, 1988.

VALDES, GIULIANO. The Land of Jesus, Bonechi & Steimatzky, Florence, Italy, 2005.

WAREHAM, NORMAN and GILL, JILL. *Pilgrim Guide to the Holy Land Gospel Sites*, McCabe Travel, London, 1992.

WILKINSON, JOHN. *Egreria's Travels*, Aris and Phillips Ltd, Warminster, England, 2002.